Lasell Junior College Library
Auburndale, Massachusetts

Presented by

Mrs. Charles A. Thompson
In Memoriam
Charles A. Thompson

DEGAS

SPRING ART BOOKS

Degas

BY PHOEBE POOL

SPRING BOOKS • LONDON

ACKNOWLEDGEMENTS

The paintings in this volume are reproduced by kind permission of the following galleries and collections to which they belong: Musée des Beaux-Arts, Algiers (Plate 39); Barber Institute of Fine Arts, Birmingham (Plate 29); Musée Bonnat, Bayonne (Plate 7); Museum of Fine Arts, Boston (Plate 23); Bührle Collection, Zürich (Plate 12); Sir William Burrell Collection, Glasgow (Plates 34, 35, 38, 45); Art Institute, Chicago (Plate 42); Courtauld Collection, London (Plate 17); Cummings Collection, Chicago (Plate 48); Musée du Louvre, Paris (Plates 1, 2, 4, 8, 11, 14, 16, 18, 21, 22, 26, 28, 32, 33, 41, 43, 46); Musée de Lyon (Plate 30); McIlhenny Collection, Philadelphia (Plates 25, 37); Metropolitan Museum of Art, New York (Plates 10, 27, 44); Minneapolis Institute of Arts (Plate 13); National Gallery, London (Plates 3, 6, 31, 36, 47); National Gallery of Art, Washington, D.C. (Plate 19); Musée de Pau (Plate 20); Smith College Museum of Art, Northampton, Mass. (Plate 5); Tate Gallery, London (Plates 24, 40); Gulbenkian Collection (Frontispiece).

The paintings reproduced on plates 7, 9, 12, 15, 20, 39, 48 were photographed by Photographie Giraudon, Paris; those on plates 3, 6, 17, 24, 29, 31, 36, 40, 47 were photographed by Michael Holford, London; those on plates 1, 2, 4, 8, 11, 12, 14, 16, 18, 21, 26, 28, 32, 33, 41, 43, 46 were photographed by Jacqueline Hyde, Paris.

All paintings are © S.P.A.D.E.M., Paris, 1963.

First published 1963
Second impression 1966

Published by
SPRING BOOKS
Drury House • Russell Street • London WC2
© Paul Hamlyn Ltd 1963
Printed in Czechoslovakia by Svoboda, Prague
T 1640

CONTENTS

	Page
Introduction	7
Outline Biography of Degas	28
Some Observations on Art by Degas	32
Notes on the Plates	37
The Plates	45—92

1. Self-portrait with charcoal holder
2. Portrait of René-Hilaire de Gas
3. The young Spartans
4. The Belleli family
5. The daughter of Jepthah
6. Princess Pauline de Metternich
7. Portrait of Léon Bonnat
8. Scene of war in the Middle Ages *or* The disasters befalling the city of Orleans
9. The meet
10. The woman with chrysanthemums
11. The orchestra of the Paris Opéra
12. Mme Camus at the piano
13. Portrait of Hortense Valpinçon as a child
14. Degas' father listening to Pagans
15. Mlle Dobigny
16. Mlle Marie Dihau
17. The woman at the window
18. The woman with the vase of flowers
19. Mrs William Bell *or* Mme René de Gas
20. The cotton market, New Orleans
21. The pedicure
22. The dance foyer at the Opéra, Rue le Peletier
23. Carriage at the races
24. Head of a woman
25. Interior (The Rape)
26. Rehearsal of a ballet on the stage
27. Pouting
28. Absinthe
29. Mlle Malo
30. Café-concert at the Ambassadeurs
31. At the sea-side: little girl having her hair combed by her nurse
32. Women at a café: evening
33. Dancer bowing with a bouquet
34. The rehearsal
35. Edmond Duranty
36. Miss Lola at the Cirque Fernando
37. Miss Cassatt at the Louvre
38. Jockeys in the rain
39. Woman putting on her corset
40. Bed-time
41. Two laundresses
42. The tub
43. The milinery shop
44. At the Tuileries: the woman with the umbrella
45. The morning toilet
46. Woman combing her hair
47. Combing the hair
48. Russian dancer

BLACK AND WHITE ILLUSTRATIONS

		Page
	Frontispiece: *Self-portrait*	
1	*Sémiramis building a city*, oil on canvas	9
2	*Study for the portrait of James Tissot*, drawing	10
3	*Dancer with one leg raised*, bronze	11
4	*Ballet dancer dressed*, bronze cast from original wax	12
5	*Horse clearing an obstacle*, bronze	12

INTRODUCTION

Edgar Degas was one of the most original and experimental artists of the nineteenth century, although emotionally and politically he was a conservative and deeply soaked in the classical tradition of painting. Compared with the dramatic lives of Gauguin and Van Gogh his career seems tranquil, but there is a certain tragedy in the stages by which the young and vulnerable romantic of his early note-books became a blind misanthrope stumbling about Paris during the bombardments of the First World War. Yet the work, solely for which he lived, is neither tragic nor incomplete, and Sickert described him as having 'the good nature and high spirits that attend a sense of great power exercised in the proper channel ... a boxer who gets in blow after blow exactly as he intends'. There were other paradoxes in his life and art. He supported the Impressionists, exhibited with them and, like them, strove to catch the fleeting reality of the contemporary world, but his emphasis on drawing, form and the need for artifice and composition in a picture was completely alien to them. He was far less interested in nature than they were and more attracted by urban surroundings, artificial light and the human figure in motion. The Goncourt brothers, who were often spiteful about their contemporaries, including Degas, admitted that of all those seeking to represent modern life he had best caught its essential spirit.

Degas was born in Paris in 1834, the eldest child of a cultured banker who had considerable influence on his son's formation. His mother came from New Orleans; she died when he was a child, but the family retained links with her birthplace and Degas went there in 1872 on a memorable visit. From the age of eleven to eighteen he attended the Lycée Louis le Grand where he had a solid classical education, his best subjects being Latin, Greek, History and Recitation. This probably affected such pictures as *The young Spartans* (plate 3), with its feeling for the fresh, idyllic aspect of the ancient world, and enabled Degas to criticise the fashionable painter Gerôme's *Phryné* as pornographic because, he said, Gerôme had not understood the logical and realistic spirit of the Greeks. When he was old, Degas' niece reports that he could still read Theocritus and Virgil in the original; his French favourites included Racine, Pascal, La Rochefoucauld, Gautier, Flaubert and Hérédia, to whom he dedicated one of his sonnets. Degas' feeling for a certain classical nobility is apparent here and in his remark on the age of Louis XIV: 'They were dirty perhaps, but they were distinguished; we are clean, but we are common.' His originality lay partly in applying this sense of grandeur and balance not to stale, rhetorical subjects but to novelties which were sometimes startling — a trapeze artist, a cotton exchange, women washing or having a pedicure.

While Degas was still a schoolboy, his father used to take him to visit museums and to see the collections of family friends, such as Lacaze and Marcille, who owned good drawings by Prudhon, Chardin and Fragonard, and Valpinçon who brought about Degas' meeting with Ingres, whom he revered all his life. Later, Degas often told how Valpinçon had refused to lend to Ingres for exhibition his celebrated *Odalisque with a turban* until persuaded by the indignation of young Degas. The collector took the painter with him to inform Ingres of his change of mind. During their visit Ingres slipped and fell fainting to the floor, and Degas was able to help him. On this or another occasion Ingres advised him '*Faites des lignes et des lignes*', and drawing, in fact, remained so much the centre of his art that in old age, when discouraging a friend in advance from giving him a pompous oration, he conceded, 'You might just say he loved drawing'. Another collector and friend of the family, Prince Gregorio Soutzo, taught Degas engraving and had long conversations with him about art, which were recorded enthusiastically in the note-books.

It was on Soutzo's advice that Degas, after abandoning the career of law, went to study with Louis Lamothe, a pupil of Ingres' disciples the Flandrins, and himself a loyal, somewhat limited, follower of the same academic tradition. Here, and for a short while at the Ecole des Beaux-Arts in 1855, Degas laid the foundation of his technique, his purity of line and feeling for the grand masses and general design of a picture. At this time, he drew many portraits of himself (e.g. plate 1) and his brothers and sisters, René bending over a paint-box, Achille in the uniform of a marine cadet and a very Ingres-like head of his sister Thérèse, now in the Fogg Museum; these show considerable assurance in their realism and bold, incisive outlines. In painting he used low tones, probably out of deference to Ingres, who in theory at least had distrusted bright colours. He made careful copies of old masters — Mantegna, Leonardo, Holbein — in the Louvre and the print room where he enrolled himself in 1853; later in Assisi he reminded himself that he could study the Giottos more thoroughly once back in Paris. Degas' father was a gifted amateur musician, and he himself became a passionate opera-goer; orchestral players and singers were to be the subject of some of his most brilliant naturalist pictures. At the theatre he was enraptured by La Ristori playing Medea ('I saw the most adorable figure from the Greek vases walking and talking'). His notes and drawings of her performance are one of the first signs of his later ability to seize the crucial point in a rapid movement. In general his earliest pictures are comparatively static and frieze-like, as behoved a disciple of Ingres.

1 *Sémiramis building a city*, c. 1861. Musée du Louvre, Paris. Oil on canvas, 58 × 110 in. (147 × 279 cm.).

2 *Study for the portrait of James Tissot*, c. 1861-8. Fogg Museum of Art, Harvard University, Cambridge, Massachusetts. $12\frac{1}{4} \times 13\frac{3}{4}$ in. (31×35 cm.).

3 *Dancer with one leg raised*. Marlborough Fine Arts Ltd., London. Bronze, $22\frac{5}{8}$ in. (58 cm.).

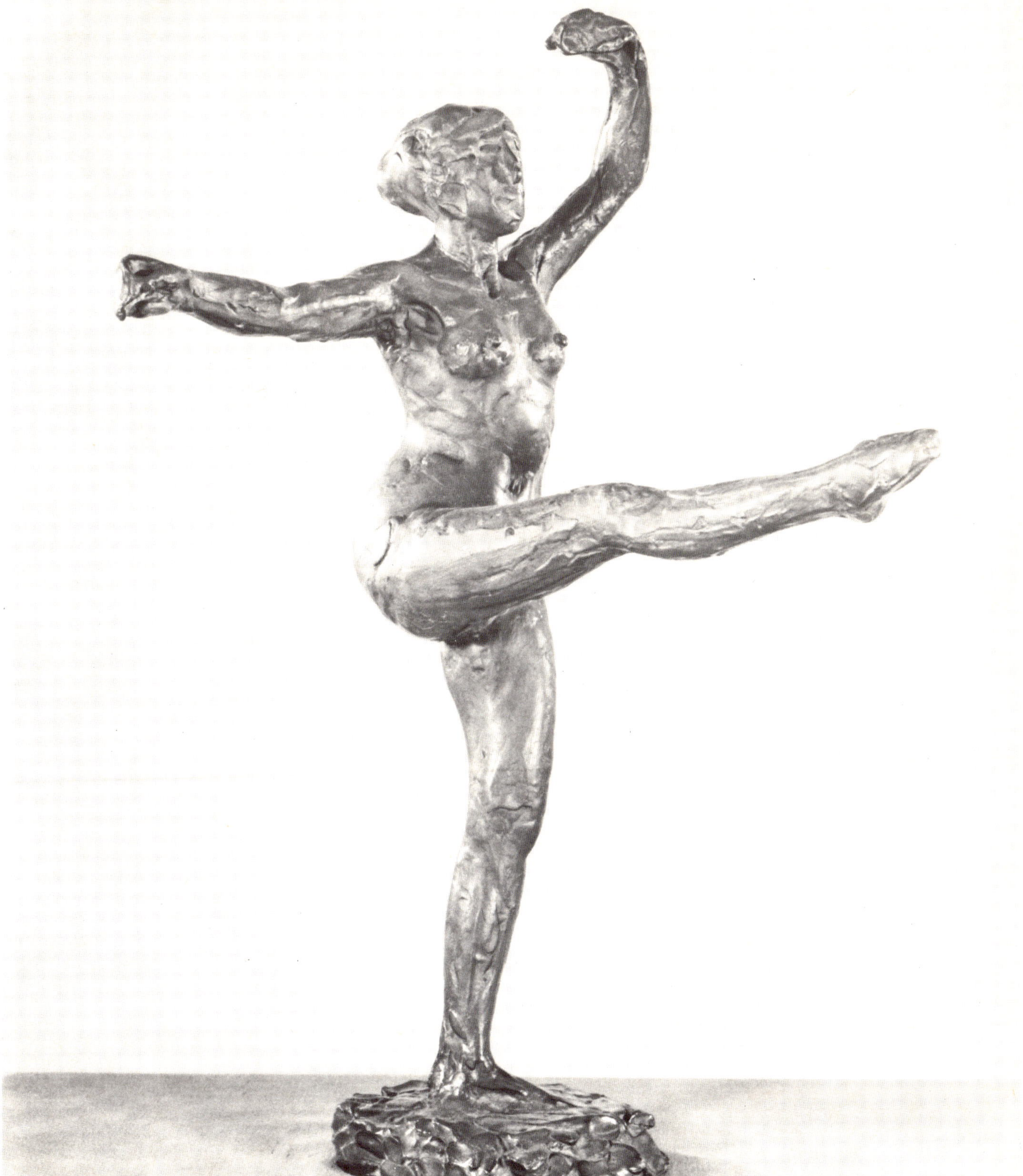

4 *Ballet dancer dressed*, c. 1880. Tate Gallery, London. Bronze cast from original wax, 39 in. (99 cm.).

5 *Horse clearing an obstacle*, c. 1881. Tate Gallery, London. Bronze, 11¼ in. (28.5 cm.).

Long visits to Italy played an essential part in the development and liberation of Degas' talent. He had been able to go there from an early age, since he had a grandfather living in Naples and an aunt in Florence. From 1857 to 1860 he was in Italy for the greater part of the year, but now his centre was Rome, where a group of his friends, old and new, were living in or near the French Academy, the Villa Médicis. The atmosphere of this little colony is well conveyed by the letters of the composer Honoré Bizet, who was then a *pensionnaire* (a prize-winner given a grant by the government to live at the Academy) and by the novelist and playwright Edmond About, who stayed in the Villa Médicis to write his *Rome Contemporain*, published in 1861. Except for About, they seem to have taken little interest in politics, but there was considerable interchange among those practising different arts. They formed a society, the Cal d'arrosti, which met in the Café Greco to talk about artistic ideas. Although the group was romantic in the *exalté* manner of the young and often chose exotic and medieval themes (Bizet had just written a cantata called *Clovis et Clothilde*), they naturally could not contemplate being Romantics after the pattern of Hugo and Delacroix in the 1830's. We know that Bizet considered Lamartine too self-dramatising, and that Degas, like Gautier and the Parnassians in Paris, soon developed an almost scientific exactitude and power of effacing himself behind his work. His own particular friends, whom he had known at the Ecole des Beaux-Arts, were the engraver Tourny and Léon Bonnat and Elié Delaunay who later became successful academic painters.

Probably more important to Degas was Gustave Moreau, a literary and mythological painter, later an idol of the Symbolists, who was more sophisticated and intelligent than the others. He had been working with Delacroix's pupil Chassériau, and seems to have directed Degas' attention to the animated, colourful and painterly art of Delacroix and the Venetians. Years later Bonnat declared that they had all been mad on Moreau. Degas' father seems to have perceived his son's admiration at the time, for, in the autumn of 1858 he wrote grumbling that he was sure Gustave Moreau's presence in Florence would delay Edgar's return to Paris. In other letters he said that he did not share his son's admiration for Delacroix, but he noticed with satisfaction that he had freed himself from the trivial and flabby drawing of Flandrin and Lamothe and from dull grey colours.

The result of these new admirations can be seen in Degas' *The daughter of Jepthah* (plate 5) and perhaps still more in the sketches, notes and reminders he made for himself while planning it. Unlike the calmer, more Ingres-like *The young Spartans* (plate 3) or *Sémiramis founding a city*, where the figures are grouped on horizontal lines, the movements of the characters in *Jepthah* were intended to suggest drama ('the group of women round the girl surround her with frightened motions'); nothing was to be static, even a small hill must be like a wave. The stuffed-looking horse in *Sémiramis* is abandoned and almost becomes the plunging steed beloved of Delacroix, perhaps borrowed from his *Justice of Trajan*, which Degas copied. Degas' notes on colour at this time refer often to Delacroix and Veronese, e.g. 'For the red of Jepthah's robe, remember the orange-reds of the old man in the Delacroix painting', and (in front of the mosaics in the Naples Museum), 'Really, I know nothing which gives the effect of this harmony better than a beautiful vivid Veronese grey, like silver and as if covered with blood'. It was scarcely to be expected that Lamothe would approve of this conversion to the opposite camp, and in January 1859 a letter of Tourny alludes to a breach between Degas and his old master.

But in Italy Degas was also educating himself by a method that Ingres, Lamothe and his father thoroughly approved — by copying old masters and particularly works of the early Renaissance. A taste for the painters before Raphael was not yet widespread in France but was more or less confined to the followers of Ingres who had initiated it. Delacroix, for instance, believed that deliberately to cultivate what he called 'the dryness of the primitives' was like grown men imitating the speech and gestures of childhood. It is possible here that Degas and Delaunay suggested this practice to Gustave Moreau, for he too copied a great number of the same painters, including Fra Angelico, Signorelli, Mantegna, Bellini, Giotto, Gozzoli, Perugino, and some of his studies seem to have been done at roughly the same time as those of Degas — e.g. a sketch from Donatello's *St George* at Orsanmichele, Florence. A note-book of Degas records a trip he made from Rome to Florence in the summer of 1858 and reveals his intoxication at seeing Orvieto and Assisi. But he also loved and studied the masters of the High Renaissance — del Sarto, Titian, Michelangelo and above all Leonardo whose subtlety and intellectualism were no doubt particularly congenial to him. From the Italian masters Degas probably took the Umbrian ovals of his women's heads, the effect produced by a suspended motion, the use of angular, tortured silhouettes. Probably too the works of Raphael and Titian gave him some justification for cutting off part of a figure by the picture frame, a practice wrongly attributed to his study of Japanese art, since he was doing it before he knew the latter. Degas copied nudes by Michelangelo, though he seemed less interested in anatomy and more in the tensions of the skin, more inclined to particular detail and less to synthesis than was Michelangelo. The supple drawing for the kneeling figure in *Sémiramis* (see figure 1), the delicate tonal shading in the studies for *The disasters of the town of Orleans* show how far the old masters had taken him from the tight Ingres-like line of the early works.

Degas must have felt some contradiction between the claims of the old masters and his absorption in the life around him, for later, on his return from Italy, he wrote 'O Giotto don't prevent me from seeing Paris, and you Paris don't prevent me from seeing Giotto'. One may suspect Moreau's influence in the fact that during the years of their closest friendship Degas planned and partly executed nearly all the history pictures he ever painted; at no other time in his life did he show a comparable neglect of the contemporary world, which for Moreau always remained without interest. But even then Degas did not altogether abandon modernity. While working on *The young Spartans* he removed various 'classical' details — antique bonnets and a temple — from his early studies and changed the noble classical profiles of the Greek girls to 'Montmartre types' with snub noses, so that in the final version they look like forerunners of his little dancing girls, with the same immature bodies. The feeling which prompted this is perhaps illuminated by a later letter, now generally ascribed to Degas, quoted in his friend Duranty's *La Nouvelle Peinture* (1877). The painter declared that it was strange how artists whose own wives or mistresses were slim and light with retroussé noses, were constantly unfaithful to them by putting sombre, strong and regular featured Grecian women into their pictures. Degas' history pictures are all more 'modern' than those of his fashionable contemporaries, such as Gerôme and Bouguereau, who were apt to overload their works with an appalling litter of archaeological details, usually incorrect.

In Rome Degas also painted various genre subjects including the well-known *Roman beggar-woman* and the *Old Italian woman with a yellow shawl*. In choosing these themes, he may have been influenced by the example of Victor Schnetz, Director of the French Academy, who apparently took some of the young men on expeditions to study Italian popular life — pilgrimages, carnivals and so on. When young himself, Schnetz had struck up a friendship with the ill-starred painter Léopold Robert, and together they used to paint the beautiful wives of some captured brigands, who were immured in the Baths of Diocletian. Although Degas was not living in the Villa Médicis himself, Schnetz had many contacts with young French painters outside and often invited them to his parties. Degas' friends Delaunay and Bonnat, both *pensionnaires*, also painted genre.

More important and original works are the well-known portrait of the Belleli family (plate 4) and one less famous which, however, preceded it, that of Mme Ducros, a friend of his brother in New Orleans, which was painted on a visit to Italy. The pictures are contrary to all the conventions of portraiture at the time in that both show a man with his back turned; in the family portrait, it is Degas' uncle, Baron Belleli himself, the head of the family, and the centre of the picture is devoted only to a table, in front of which sits the youngest girl in a nonchalant pose with her foot up on the chair. To achieve this deceptively casual effect, Degas made many studies, and he probably learnt something from contemporary developments in photography. Earlier processes, such as daguerreotypes demanded long, stationary poses which tended to fix the model in conventional attitudes, but the advent of instantaneous photography about this time made it possible to seize life in all its spontaneity. There are even contemporary photographs in which the main figure of a group has his back turned in the same way, e.g. one by F. Lincke, showing the Russian ambassador in Berlin with his family.

At first sight the Belleli family has some resemblance to a portrait group painted a little earlier by Degas' friend Léon Bonnat, but the treatment of light is more subtle in the Degas; there are less violent contrasts and more attention is given to the surface of the picture. Manet sometimes claimed that he had been painting scenes of contemporary life when Degas was still occupied with *Sémiramis*, but the portrait of Manet's parents, compared with the Belleli family, seems staid and conventional, and it was painted after Degas' group. A jotting in Degas' note-book of 1859—60 shows what he was trying to do at the time when the Belleli portrait was being planned. 'M. Beaucousin's Arioste appeals to me very much, but it remains to find a composition which depicts our time.' In Italy he had also written, 'I am going to steep myself in the movement of Paris; there is no telling what will happen but I shall always be honest.' He was already prepared for his new friendships with Duranty and Manet whom he probably met about 1862—3 when he was making an engraving from Velasquez' *Infanta* in the Louvre.

It is certain that the subjects of Degas' great naturalistic pictures owe a great deal to the climate of his age. It would have been impossible for a contemporary of Delacroix and Ingres to have painted a woman having a pedicure for example, and difficult to imagine a man of Picasso's generation doing so, since they were also hostile to such realism. Degas recognised this himself when he said that in an earlier age he would have painted Susanna and the Elders, instead of women washing themselves. What then were the chief forces in the intellectual atmosphere which drove the new generation of the sixties towards realism?

The second half of the nineteenth century was an age dominated by science, an age in which the subjectivity and vague idealisation of the Romantics was being replaced by more exact observation and by an impersonal approach. The impact of science can be traced everywhere from Taine's way of writing history to the new detective stories of Gaboriau, whose detective Le Coq used a pseudo-scientific vocabulary and methods like a naturalist 'who from one or two bones could draw the animal from which they came'. The Goncourt brothers, whom Degas knew, relied on close observation and documentation for their novels; they visited hospitals, collected the letters of prostitutes and constructed their novel about a young girl from the confidences of actual young girls. This is somewhat like Degas' projects, in the note-books, to make a series of pictures on different kinds of mourning, different sorts of bread and to study corsets which still retained the shape of the body. In both cases, too, the subjects of their study were everyday ones, often sordid, in comparison with the lofty themes of Ingres and Delacroix. Since Courbet, painters no longer regarded man as more divine and heroic than the objects round him, and they claimed the same power of neutral, unheightened lack of selection for their subject as that of a mirror. Degas, Manet and the naturalist writers all felt that they should depict the contemporary scene, often the life of Paris itself, as Baudelaire advocated in *Le Peintre de la vie moderne*. Men such as Maxime du Camp wrote poems on industry, the Suez Canal and the new transatlantic cable, while Manet painted a concert in the Tuileries Gardens, and Degas showed Viscount Lepic and his children crossing the Place de la Concorde.

Degas is perhaps the only great painter of his generation who was not directly affected by the influence of Courbet, but when he began to meet Manet and his friends in the Café Guerbois on the Boulevard de Clichy, he was entering the circle of Courbet's spiritual heirs. Courbet had dared to paint the ordinary incidents of his own countryside and life, e.g. *After dinner at Ornans*, and *The burial at Ornans*, as if they had the same importance as the legends of antiquity, and in *The studio* (1855) he had made a modern allegory using characters such as Baudelaire, who had determined his own development. Courbet, too, had said 'The beauty given by nature is superior to all the artistic conventions', and 'The painter must only paint what is before his eyes'. But in several respects the friends at the Café Guerbois differed from the earlier group around Courbet, which had been humanitarian and affected by the teaching of the socialist Prudhon. Degas was most certainly not left-wing, and his friend Duranty took a rather snobbish care to distinguish his movement from the Bohemian *sans-culottes* of earlier realism. Although some writers have claimed that Manet was a radical, in the *Music in the Tuileries* he seems to have represented himself and his friends as upper-class dandies and introduced such fashionable figures as Lord Taylor in order to identify his own group with the aristocratic onlookers in a picture by Velasquez.

At the Café Guerbois, besides Manet, Degas met Renoir, Pissarro, Monet, Sisley, Fantin-Latour, occasionally Cézanne and Zola and above all, Edmond Duranty, the theorist of the movement and author of *Réalisme* and *La Nouvelle Peinture*. Duranty believed that artists should always seek 'to show the social side of a man, which is the most visible, comprehensible and varied aspect', and that the representation even of a man's back should make it possible to deduce his age, social status and temperament. He wanted 'to take down the wall which separated the studio from the life of the day'. In some of his novels, such as *Le Peintre Louis Martin*, he has introduced imaginary artists alongside the real ones, including Degas, of whom he wrote, 'He is an artist of rare intelligence, preoccupied with ideas, which seems strange to the majority of his fellow-artists.' When the fictional Louis Martin attacked Poussin, Duranty made Degas defend him, characteristically pointing out his purity of drawing, amplitude of modelling and grandeur of disposition.

Although Degas was always somewhat reserved and solitary, these evenings at the

Café Guerbois preserved him from isolation and put him in touch with painters more sympathetic to his own aims than his academic friends at the Villa Médicis. Manet had a great distaste for the cloudy and metaphysical; his greatest expression of contempt was, 'What! do you take me for a history painter?' He naturally disapproved of Moreau, of whom he said, 'He goes in a bad direction. He leads us to the unknown, we who wish everything to be understood', and in a note-book of *c.* 1863—7 Degas himself refers to Moreau's painting as dilettantism. Degas' friendship with Manet was often stormy, particularly when the latter cut away part of a portrait which Degas had done of his wife and himself, and later when Manet refused to exhibit with the Impressionists. Nevertheless, in 1869 one finds Manet lending Baudelaire's *Les Fleurs du Mal* to Degas, and one is reminded that these two well-educated and witty men had far more in common than they had with Renoir or Monet whose origins were more humble. In their work, too, they were both trying to develop an informal composition which would nevertheless be tightly organised on the surface of the picture. The greater freedom of colour and handling in Degas' works at this time probably owes much to Manet, and certainly the latter in his *La Musique aux Tuileries* (1862) and *Déjeuner sur l'herbe* had achieved part of Degas' ambition 'to find a composition which represents our time'. Degas, however, was more economical in his means and never crowded his canvas as tightly as *La Musique aux Tuileries*.

From about 1869 to 1880, the subject matter of Degas' art was very wide; these were the years of his great naturalist masterpieces, in which he often managed to convey, as Duranty demanded, the particular setting of a person in his social milieu — the brothers Degas in their office, Rouart in front of his factory or Mlle Dihau (*c.* 1869) with her little suitcase as an emblem to show that she was often in transit between Paris and Lille. He became interested, as he wrote, 'in doing portraits of people in familiar and typical attitudes and in giving the face the same kind of expression as the body'. A splendid example of this period, showing Degas' sister Thérèse Morbille embroidering while her husband talks to her, his leg propped on the back of the sofa (*c.* 1866), seems to have left the perfectionist Degas dissatisfied, for he erased part of it and kept it forgotten in his studio. At this time he also painted *Mme Camus at the piano* (plate 12) and *Portrait of Hortense Valpinçon as a child* (plate 13), both of which give the effect of their sitters having halted for a moment in their ordinary lives rather than of posing formally for a portrait, and so does the picture of *Degas and Valernes*, who seem to be arguing in a studio against a sea of Paris roofs. Degas was extremely interested in artificial light, but unlike his contemporaries, he generally used it to clarify rather than to dissolve the contours of his figure. His picture *Mme Camus in red*, painted about 1870, apparently a study of firelight, is probably one of the results of his resolution in one of the note-books: 'To work a great deal at evening effects, lamps, candles etc. The fascinating thing is not to show the source of light but the effect of light. That side of art today could become immense — is it possible not to see it?'

Degas' interest in horse-racing probably dates from about 1860 when he visited M. and Mme Paul Valpinçon in Normandy, delighting in the very green grass which, he said, was like England. He developed his skill at portraying horses very rapidly from the gaucherie of his early, wooden and incorrect *Wounded jockey* (1866) to the wonderful *Carriage at the races* (*c.* 1873; plate 23). In his later studies of horses, he used the photographs of Major Muybridge to give a truthful effect of movement. *Jockeys in the rain* (*c.* 1881; plate 38) is one of his most monumental treatments of this subject. These were the years, too, when he became interested in music and musicians as a theme for painting, although the note for a series on instruments (their shape, the twist of hand, arm and neck of a violinist, for example, the swelling and hollowing of a bassoonist's cheeks) is somewhat later. Through his friend Dihau, a bassoonist at the Opéra, Degas came to know the whole orchestra which he painted in his celebrated picture of *c.* 1869 (plate 11). Another masterpiece of this time shows his father listening to the singer Pagans (plate 14).

Degas had been one of the first to share the enthusiasm of his friend the engraver Bracquemond for the art of Hokusai. About 1862—3 Mme Desoye, who had lived in Japan, opened her shop 'La Jonque Chinoise' in the Rue de Rivoli, and artists and writers, including Baudelaire, the Goncourts, Whistler, Duranty and Degas, flocked to see and buy her prints. After the Franco-Prussian war it became still easier to obtain Japanese *objets d'art*. Degas seems to have relished their steep foreshortenings, their asymmetrical compositions, their sober colour, flatness and new viewpoints. Japanese influence can be seen in such work as *Two dancers resting*, now in Boston, but on the whole it confirmed him in his own experiments rather than originally suggesting them to him.

As early as 1866—8 Degas had painted ballet, but this picture of Mlle Fiocre in *La source* has more links with the exotic history pictures than with the realism of his later ballet scenes. It does, however, give a clue to one reason for Degas' obsession — ballet has a magical quality of romance and ritual without being of those legendary or historical subjects so much despised by Manet and his friends. The subject also provided him with opportunities for showing strange effects of light and, above all, the struggle of tensed bodies to obtain perfection, a theme which also attracted him to acrobats and laundresses. (It has been pointed out that the French ballet was not at the period of its greatest splendour when Degas painted it, but this decline was irrelevant to his purposes.) The year 1872 marks the real beginning of Degas' preoccupation with ballet, with *The dance foyer at the Opéra, Rue le Peletier* (plate 23), and this was followed by numerous other masterpieces such as *Rehearsal of a ballet on the stage* (1874; plate 26) and the *Dancing rehearsal* (*c.* 1877). Roughly speaking, Degas, in these earliest ballet scenes, appears to be mainly interested in ensembles and actual performances, classes or rehearsals; about 1878 he concentrates more on studies of movement with individual dancers, and the last period, from 1885 onwards, is that of the big pastels with thick hatchings, which often show certain specific gestures, such as the dancer adjusting her shoulder strap or earrings. These are considerably affected by his increasing blindness.

This period marks the beginning of Degas' complete power and mastery of his craft, but it was also the time when serious personal troubles assailed him. Apart from the menace of his failing sight, the death of his father in 1874, in itself a sorrow, revealed that the bank which he had managed was in a bad financial state. When he and his brother Achille asked René to repay the money borrowed from his father to establish his cotton firm, they found not only that he could not, but that he himself needed help. Edgar and his brother-in-law Févre (Marguerite's husband) with their own money refunded the loan, which according to Mme Halévy was a debt of honour, to clear the family name, and by no means a legal obligation. Degas was, however, obliged by law to repay a large sum owed to a bank in Antwerp, and to do all this he had to work extremely hard and to sell some of his beloved collection. He was in no way a Bohemian, and though he lived ascetically, he felt embarrassed at entertaining his friends in his new, more cramped quarters. In 1878, his brother René provided a new blow by divorcing his blind wife, who was their cousin. Degas who had admired her courage and painted her, was extremely shocked; he broke with his brother and did not see him for twenty years.

The letters of Berthe Morisot and her sister during these years show Degas at parties, guarded and reserved with women (Manet, who was less shy, said Degas did not know how to talk to them at all), but easy and assured when he was actually working, so that when he was painting Berthe's sister a crowd of visitors scarcely disturbed him. But this period of growing maturity in Degas' art was roughly interrupted by the war of 1870, in which the painter served in the artillery. The loss of friends and the danger to his country naturally saddened him, although he found some compensation in the company of his old school friends, Henry and Alexis Rouart, who were by chance in the same battery. An experience of sleeping in the cold at this time is thought to have started or accelerated an injury to his eyes, which was profoundly to affect his later work.

After the war in 1872 when Degas' brother René came from Louisiana to visit his family in Paris, he took Edgar back with him. They sailed on the ship 'Scotia', the speed of which impressed the painter, but he complained of 'the coldness and conventional distrust' of the English passengers, whose language he could imitate but not speak. (Sickert tells us that one of his favourite jokes was to repeat with an execrable accent and a pleading expression, an English notice which had taken his fancy, 'Pliz, pliz, hadjust your clothes on leaving'.)

His letters from New Orleans give a poetical and accurate account of his impressions. 'I like nothing better than the Negresses of all shades, holding in their arms little white babies, so white against white houses, with columns of fluted wood and in gardens of orange trees and the ladies in muslin against the fronts of their little houses and the steamboats with two chimneys as tall as factory chimneys and the fruit-vendors with their shops full to bursting, and the contrast between the lively hum and bustle of the offices with their immense black animal force, etc. etc. And the pretty women of pure blood and the pretty twenty-five-year-olds and the well-set-up negresses!... But one Paris laundry girl, with bare arms, is worth it all for such a pronounced Parisian as I am.' Degas also wrote that Manet would find more inspiration in New Orleans than he himself could, for he believed that an artist should have roots in a country he was painting, and that without long familiarity 'the instantaneous impression is photographing and no more'. He also complained that it was difficult to get his relations or their children to take him seriously enough to sit still. Nevertheless, he managed to paint some of his most original and brilliant pictures during this visit. The nurse on duty and the children on the veranda approached by a large dog, express the same taste for the marginal, the off-beat and the refractory subject which was noticeable as early as the portrait of Mme Ducros. Such a theme as the celebrated *Cotton market, New Orleans* (plate 20) had never been painted before and rarely since. Degas also painted several delicate and more conventional portraits of Mrs William Bell and of his blind sister-in-law, René's wife Estelle (plates 18 and 19).

Back in Paris, Degas devoted himself particularly to ballet and to a rather odd kind of genre which was new to him. The 'advanced' painters of his generation were justifiably suspicious of anecdotal and literary subjects, which had become the monopoly of the fashionable academic painters, and were very popular both with the critics and the middle-class visitors to the Salon, because, without the old aristocratic connoisseurship, it was easier for them to discuss such subject-matter than the refinements of technique and composition. Nevertheless, for a short while, Degas experimented with pictures which seem to tell a story, such as the grim *Rape* or *The interior* (plate 25), *Pouting* (plate 27) and *Absinthe* (plate 28). It was probably about the same time that Degas made drawings inspired by the Goncourts' *La Fille d'Elsa*, and in 1874 the brothers' *Journal* records a visit to the painter's studio. Although there certainly seems to be a parallel between the documentary and story-telling side of Degas' art and the novels of the naturalists such as the Goncourts and Zola, Degas' niece Jeanne Fèvre records that after liking the latter, he grew tired of them and returned to his beloved classics. He did, however, continue to admire de Maupassant.

The group of painters who met at the Café Guerbois before the war of 1870 and afterwards at the Nouvelle Athènes had, for a while, received support from the dealer Durand-Ruel. But a business slump and the total incomprehension of buyers forced him to withdraw his help; nor did the Salon, re-opened in 1872, accept any of the *plein-air* artists' works, except one of Berthe Morisot's.

In May 1873 Paul Alexis, the critic, wrote in *Avenir National:* 'Like any other trade, the artist should organise at once and exhibit outside the official salon where the narrowest kind of ostracism reigns unchecked'. This was precisely what they were doing, with Degas in the leading rôle. He was better educated and knew more of the world than most of the others, except Manet, and Manet backed up by Fantin-Latour refused to compromise himself, preferring to wait for the acclaim of the official Salon. (One is reminded of Degas' remark on another occasion: 'This is not the first time I have noticed what a *bourgeois* you are, Manet.') Degas' own loyalty to the Impressionists was constant and disinterested. When the group was formed, he still had a good private income and did not care at all whether his own pictures were shown or not. Yet during the eight Impressionist exhibitions, he only refused to send his work on one occasion. He gave the group unfailing support in practical matters, and purposely invited less provocative painters, such as Boudin, Lepine and de Nittis to join them. In return for this sensible concession, the more committed Impressionists insisted on including Cézanne, whom Degas at this time disliked. When Guillemet refused to join, he was congratulated by the elderly Corot, who told him, 'You were damned right to get out, my boy'.

The history of the Impressionist movement is, of course, too long, well known and irrelevant for discussion here. At the first exhibition, which opened in April 1874, in the photographer Nadar's old studio off the Boulevard des Capuchines, Degas showed ten canvases, including *The laundress, At the races, The rehearsal* and *The false start*; they escaped the worst scorn and vituperation of the critics, presumably because their colour was more delicate than the works of Monet, Pissarro and Renoir. But then in 1876, at the second exhibition, Degas showed *The cotton market, New Orleans* and the pastel of *Estelle Musson*. Albert Wolff of the *Figaro* chose very unwise grounds on which to attack them. 'Try to make M. Degas listen to reason, tell him that in art there are certain qualities called drawing, colour, execution and will power, and he will laugh in your face and consider you a reactionary.' Fortunately Duranty published in the same year his *La Nouvelle Peinture, à propos du groupe d'artistes qui expose à la galerie Durand-Ruel*, and this was full of Degas' ideas and of praise for Degas. (This last fact is one of the reasons for no longer believing that the painter himself actually helped to write it — he was far too proud for such self-advertisement.) Among other praise of his friend, Duranty wrote, 'The series of new ideas took form in the mind of a draughtsman, one of our group, one of those who exhibit their work in these rooms, a mind and a talent the like of which is seldom encountered. Enough people have benefited from his conceptions and artistic generosity, and at last justice shall be done to him.'

Degas, like Delacroix, was passionately interested in problems of technique and keenly aware that the loss of the old, painstaking traditions of the artists' workshops obliged the modern painter to make personal experiments with many different media. Degas' medium, in fact, was always selected with deliberate intention. During the first half of his career, until nearly 1880, he generally used oil paint for the picture itself, reserving pencil, pastel or water-colour for the preparatory studies. At first he used a thin, rather dry oil paint, but later he employed brighter, thicker and richer colours. About 1875–6 he began to use pastel more and more, and from 1885 it was almost always the medium for his important works. He taught himself how to vary its texture and *matière*; he worked with pastel over monotype, as in the *Café-concert at the Ambassadeurs* and the *Women at a café* (plates 30 and 32) and combined it with other media such as gouache and water-colour. He also liked to contrast areas of dry pastel, used normally, with pastel turned into a paste by hot water and applied with a brush. Before 1880 Degas usually applied pastel smoothly in delicate subtle colours; after 1880 he made broken surface texture with emphatic hatchings and contrasting tones of sharper, brighter colours.

The decade after his return from New Orleans saw his subject-matter at its widest and perhaps most original. But after about 1886, until he had to stop working in about 1908, he confined himself almost entirely to dancers and nudes, treated with a heavier, more summary line and sculptural breadth. Some reasons for Degas' preoccupation with ballet have already been suggested, but his feelings about it and the extent to which he identified himself as an artist, consciously or not, with the dancers in their conquest of difficulty, is illuminated still more by the sonnets he wrote between 1889 and 1890. It may seem strange that Degas, who affected to despise writers in so far as they discussed painting, should seek to poach upon their field. Paul Valéry and Gide quote him as saying, 'The muses never hold discussions together; all day they work quite separately; when evening comes and work is finished, they come together and dance; they never talk'. But he also liked to pretend that all art was a matter of will, and he had been accustomed to compose little *jeux d'esprit*, limericks, etc., on social occasions. The choice of words in his note-books, letters and his oral witticisms show that he had considerable literary talent.

The immediate stimulus for Degas' sonnets seems to have been his friend Mallarmé's collection of poems *Le Tiroir de Lacque*, which he asked Degas, Renoir, Monet and Berthe Morisot to illustrate. Degas had to read it carefully, and must have admired Mallarmé's fierce struggle for formal perfection, which resembled his own. He was also influenced by the new Parnassian school of poets, particularly by Hérédia, to whom perhaps the best of Degas' sonnets was dedicated.

> *Vous n'ecorcherez point un Marsyas de peu;*
> *Lourdement de jouer un soir lui prit l'envie;*
> *Avant de regagner son ordinaire vie,*
> *Il baise et vous remet l'outil sacré du jeu.*
>
> *Inoubliable outil de dure poésie*
> *Qui vous pouvez, poète, à la forge d'un Dieu*
> *Marteler, ciseler et rougir dans le feu*
> *Pour que sa Griffe fume en le rime choisie . . .**

* Do not skin alive a man who one evening fancied playing crudely like Marsyas; before returning to his ordinary life he kisses the sacred tool and hands it back to you. Unforgettable tool of hard poetry which you, poet, at the forge of the gods, can hammer and chisel and redden in the fire to stamp it with its seal in the chosen rhyme.

Degas himself found 'the sacred tool' of poetry difficult to wield and complained that he had worked a whole day on a sonnet without advancing at all. 'And it isn't ideas which I lack. I have all too many.' Mallarmé's reply has become celebrated: 'One does not make sonnets with ideas, Degas, but with words.' It was no doubt his experience in paint and words of that eternal struggle for expression which T.E. Lawrence said 'is like trying to fight a feather bed' that gave Degas his sympathy with the ballerina poised between magic and bathos.

> *Sifflent les violons. Fraîche, du bleu de l'eau*
> *Silvana vient, et là curieuse s'ebroue*
> *Le bonheur de revivre et l'amour pur se joue*
> *Sur ses yeux, sur ses seins, sur tout l'être nouveau.*
>
> *Mais d'un signe toujours cesse le beau mystère*
> *Elle retire trop les jambes en sautant:*
> *C'est un saut de grenouille aux mares de Cythère.**

* The violins squeak. Fresh from the blue water, Silvana rises, curious and gambolling, the happiness of rebirth and pure love plays on her eyes, her breasts and all her new being. But a trifle puts to flight the mysterious beauty. Leaping, she bends her legs too far: like the leap of a frog in the ponds of Cytheraera.

This sense of triviality and failure, always in waiting to ambush painter and dancer alike, is very characteristic of Degas.

Towards the end of Degas' career, even his ballet dancers, jockeys and laundresses were outnumbered by innumerable variants on one theme — women at their toilet. Believing, like Baudelaire, that no aspect of life was too shameful to be treated in art,

Degas deliberately set out to show, not nudes posed as if radiantly conscious of an onlooker, but women cleaning themselves as if unperceived, like cats. 'Perhaps I have gone too far in treating women as animals?' Degas asked Sickert. Huysmans, who generally misunderstood matters of this sort (and even believed that Moreau was a vicious decadent), declared that Degas brought 'an attentive cruelty and a patient hatred' to his nude studies. But Huysmans had never been a close friend of Duranty, and the nudes were partly the embodiment of Duranty's naturalistic creed — that the wall separating the studio from actual life should be taken away. Besides, Degas was far from being a misogynist; he enjoyed the company of women and had many women friends. His solitude and celibacy may have resulted from some frustrating love affairs in his youth. We know from the note-books that he fell in love at least once, and also that he had hoped to marry. ('I do not know how to say how much I love that girl,' erased afterwards as much as possible, and 'Could I find a nice little wife, someone quite simple and quiet, who would understand my crazy ideas, and with whom I could live while working at what I love best.') The latter was written in Italy when he was twenty-four, but fourteen years later, in New Orleans, he still had the same hope. Perhaps it was defeated by his brother's financial troubles, or more likely there was some truth in his joke that he had not married for fear of hearing his wife say, 'That's a nice little thing that you've done this morning' — in other words his passion for his art left no room for any other close relationship.

Degas was impenetrably reserved about his relationship with women, but it is generally thought that he loved Mlle Volkonsa in vain when he was about twenty, that later he may have loved Désiré Dihau's sister, whom he called in a letter 'my cruel friend', and that some time after 1874 he almost certainly had an affair with Mary Cassatt, of whom he wrote that they had 'identical intellectual dispositions and an identical predilection for drawing'. (After he had made an acid remark to someone else about her work, she apparently refused to see him for some years.) That Degas often went to brothels, according to the Goncourts, tells us little since it was the usual practice for a bachelor of his time; his monotypes of life in such houses are objective and devoid of sensuality. But that Degas' great series of nudes (see plates 43, 44, 46) is a hymn of hate against women is sufficiently disproved by merely looking at the magnificent *The morning toilet* (plate 44), for example, which in its different way is as delicious as a Renoir. In these nudes (some of which were exhibited at the last Impressionist exhibition in 1886, under the title 'Series of female nudes, bathing, washing, drying, rubbing down, combing their hair or having it combed'), Degas progressively limited detail until the bodies gradually became transformed into generalised masses of light, which were almost exercises in pure painting. One is reminded of Monet's development from the realism of 1874 to the late water-lilies.

Enough has perhaps been said about the predominant rôle of drawing in Degas' art, but it should perhaps be mentioned in passing that his draughtsmanship evolved from 'the single line that determines a figure' taught by Ingres, to a less continual, more irregular line which was at once more agile and more vigorous, and that he abandoned lead pencil in favour of pastel.

Degas made a considerable number of statuettes, and when he died about 150 pieces were found in his studio, many of them broken. A knowledge of the secrets of mass helped him as a painter, and later, when his eyes failed and he could neither paint nor draw, he could still mould and knead the clay or wax. His sculptures were done, even more than his other works, to please himself, and he only exhibited one, *Ballet dancer dressed*, in 1881 (see figure 4). As early as 1868—70, Degas executed a bas-relief called *Young girls gathering apples*, which he allowed to fall into dust, but not before Renoir had seen it and acclaimed Degas as 'our foremost sculptor'. During the siege of Paris, he met the animal sculptor Cuvelier and was stimulated by his work to make numerous studies of horses, between four and twelve inches high, which are rendered with a fidelity which came partly from scrutinising the photographs of Muybridge. After the horses Degas naturally turned to dancers — generally executed in bronze, a little bigger than the horses and often showing, with great exactitude, a momentary pause between two actions.

Apart from his growing blindness, Degas' later days were saddened by the Dreyfus case, which led him to separate himself from his Jewish, and pro-Dreyfus friends, even including the Halévys, whom he had known nearly all his life. His great friend Rouart died, and so did his old and trusted house-keeper Zoë, who used to read aloud to him; finally he was forced to move from his studio to the unfamiliar Boulevard de Clichy. But although Degas lived in self-imposed and lordly seclusion, he knew about some of the younger artists, who in their turn not only knew about, but revered, him. He owned works by Forain, Toulouse-Lautrec, Gauguin, Suzanne Valadon and, less predictably, Van Gogh. It is pleasant to record these strangely different artists saluting each other from their alien temperaments, and Van Gogh writing to Emile Bernard, 'Why do you say that Degas hasn't much physical passion?... Degas' painting is virile and rightly impersonal, because privately he's resigned to being nothing but a small lawyer with a horror of the gay life.' All these artists owed much to Degas, as did Bonnard, Vuillard, Dufy and even Picasso, who had an equally original power of invention, and the same passion for Ingres' drawing and some of Degas' themes — theatres, races, brothels and such low cafés as Degas showed in *Absinthe*.

Pissarro told his son that Degas was the greatest of the moderns, and Valéry described him as 'retiring in himself, with himself... to make himself secretly, studiously and jealously incomparable?' Duranty wrote of him, 'It is necessary to have great genius to set down simply and surely what one sees before one's eyes.' In front of his musical and harmonious compositions, from which all fussy inessentials have been removed, one is reminded of the praise given to Stendhal: '*Comme il insiste peu!*' But the final word should be Degas' own. He had always wandered about Paris, refusing to take cabs, and there is something tragic and heroic in the way that he continued to do this during the war, when he was old and blind, for as he said rather fiercely, 'We are made to look at each other, aren't we.'

OUTLINE BIOGRAPHY OF DEGAS

1834 — 19th July. Edgar Degas born 8 Rue Saint-Georges, Paris, the eldest of five children. His father Pierre-Auguste-Hyacinthe de Gas managed a branch of the family bank owned by Edgar's grandfather in Naples, where the latter had fled from the Revolution. Edgar's mother was of Creole origin from New Orleans.

1845 — Entered the Lycée Louis le Grand, where he met two lifelong friends, Henri Rouart and Paul de Valpinçon.

1847 — Death of his mother.

1853 — Having passed his *baccalauréat* with success, he enrolled in the law school, but spent much time drawing and frequenting the studio of Barrias, a mediocre painter. He also enrolled in the print-room of the Bibliothèque Nationale, where he made copies of works by Mantegna, Dürer, Raphael, etc. His family had now moved to the Rue Mondivi.

1854 — First trip to Naples. In Paris, frequented the studio of Lamothe, a disciple of Ingres, who taught him drawing.

1855 — Lamothe introduced him to the Ecole des Beaux-Arts where he met Léon Bonnat, Fantin-Latour, Elié Delaunay and the engraver Tourny. This was also probably the time when he met Ingres. Visit to Italy and the South of France.

1856 — Another visit to Italy where he made an etching of Tourny. In Paris influenced by the painter and collector Soutzo, a friend of his family.

1857 — Spent much of the year in Italy (Rome) where he frequented the circle, centring round the Villa Médicis, which included Gustave Moreau, Bizet, Bonnat and Tourny. Also visited Naples, where he painted his grandfather, and Florence, where he made copies of old masters, e.g. Masaccio.

1858 — Expedition from Rome to Florence in a *voiturin*. In August and the autumn, he stayed with the Belleli family in Florence and made sketches for the family portrait.

1859 — Returned to Paris in April and worked in studio, found by his family, in the Rue Madame. Made studies for the Belleli portrait and history pictures.

1860–2	Discovered Japanese art. Visit to Valpinçons at Ménil-Hubert in Normandy and first studies of horses in movement. Probably met Manet.
1865	Showed *Scene of war in the Middle Ages* at the Salon and was congratulated by Puvis de Chavannes. For next five years sent works to Salon, but they were often refused. Began to go to the Café Guerbois near the Place Clichy, the rendezvous of Manet, Zola, Renoir, Monet and the critic Duranty, who became Degas' friend and admirer.
1866	Gave up history pictures. Exhibited *The wounded jockey* at Salon.
1868	Exhibited at Salon *Mlle Fiocre in the ballet 'La source'*, the first sign of his growing interest in theatre and ballet.
1869–70	Portraits, paintings of musicians, and horses and jockeys. Visited Boulogne and Saint Valéry-en-Caux with Manet. Executed small landscapes from memory.
1870	The last time he exhibited at Salon. During the Franco-Prusian War, served in an artillery unit of the Garde Nationale. His eyesight was affected by the cold.
1871	During the Commune, stayed at Ménil-Hubert with Valpinçons; painted their children.
1872	Began visiting the opera house of the Rue le Peletier. In October he accompanied his brother René back to New Orleans, where both his brothers were cotton merchants. He stayed there until the following April and did many portraits of the family. He also made the studies for his famous *Cotton market* picture, now at Pau.
1873	On his return to Paris, Degas lived at 77 Rue Blanche. Went often to the opera, but in the autumn the opera house was destroyed by fire. The friends who had met at the Café Guerbois now went to the Nouvelle-Athènes, where they were joined by Forain, George Moore and Desboutin. Began to paint naturalistic genre pictures, such as *Pedicure* and *Pouting*. In December, went to Turin where his father had fallen seriously ill.
1874	In February his father died at Naples. The bank which he had controlled was found to be in a difficult situation financially. Degas took a prominent part in organising the first exhibition of the Impressionists called *Première exposition de la Societé Anonyme des artistes peintres, sculpteurs, graveurs*, which opened on April 15th at the photographer Nadar's former studio. Edmond de Goncourt visited Degas' studio and commented in his journal.
1875	Had already made a considerable collection of old masters and was now forced to sell part of it, especially pastels by La Tour, to help his brother René.
1876	Second Impressionist exhibition at Durand-Ruel's gallery. Degas showed twenty-four works. Mainly venomous reviews, except that by Duranty who wrote a brochure on the new group.

1877	Moved to 4 Rue Frochot. Third Impressionist exhibition. Showed twenty-four works.
1878	*The cotton market, New Orleans*, bought by the Pau Museum, was Degas' first work to be shown in a museum.
1879	Fourth Impressionist exhibition. Degas persuaded his friends to call themselves instead the 'Independents'. Besides oil paintings and pastels, of which he was doing an increasing number, Degas exhibited decorated fans.
1880	Fifth Impressionist exhibition which was, for the first time, reviewed by the *Gazette des Beaux-Arts*. Visit to Spain. Did etchings with Mary Cassatt and Pissarro.
1881	Sixth Impressionist exhibition. Showed his first piece of sculpture, *Ballet dancer dressed*. Major Muybridge's photographs published in *Le Globe* showed Degas the real movements of galloping horses.
1882	In July, went to Etretat with Halévy and in September to Switzerland. He did not participate in the seventh Impressionist exhibition. About this time began his first series of *Milliners* and *Laundresses*.
1883	Continued to see his Impressionist friends, who now met at the Café de la Rochefoucauld. Durand-Ruel organised an Impressionist exhibition in London. Manet died.
1884	Holiday trip in August to Normandy, to his friends the Valpinçons. Made a bust of Hortense Valpinçon, which was accidentally destroyed. Met Gauguin.
1885	Eyesight worse, but still dined out often. Impressionist exhibition in Brussels. In August, visited Le Havre and Mont Saint Michel.
1886	In January visit to Naples, on family business. Installed in new apartment, 21 Rue Pigalle. The eighth and last Impressionist exhibition was held; Degas showed 'Series of women bathing, washing, drying, combing their hair'. Gave Durand-Ruel the exclusive rights to his works; the latter arranged an exhibition in New York of the Impressionist painters.
1887	Went to Spain and then Morocco.
1890	Visited his brother Achille in Geneva, and Burgundy with Bartholomé the sculptor. Took great interest in collecting pictures.
1892	Eyesight weakening. Practically abandoned oil painting. August at Ménil-Hubert with the Valpinçons where he did two studies of the billiard-room.

1893	First one-man show at Durand-Ruel's; exhibited landscapes. On the death of Caillebotte, Degas' pictures were the only ones all accepted in the Caillebotte legacy to the Luxembourg, whereas pictures of Renoir, Manet and Cézanne were refused. Trip to Interlaken and visit to Valernes at Carpentras.
1895–8	Numerous *Women bathing* and *Dancers*.
1896	In spite of bad health, went to the funeral of Valernes at Carpentras.
1897	Went for a cure at the Mont-Doré, and with Bartholomé paid a visit to the Ingres Museum at Montaubon.
1898	Stayed at Saint Valery-sur-Somme where he met his brother René, from whom he had been estranged for many years. Photographed landscapes and then drew or painted them.
1900	Contributed two paintings and five pastels to the Centennial Exhibition.
1904–6	Could now work only on large compositions or sculptures. Sometimes painted on one of his old canvases. Lived a very secluded life.
1907	Visited the Vosges mountains for his health.
1909	Could paint very little and was apparently indifferent to his growing fame.
1912	Much saddened by the death of Henri Rouart, whose collection of pictures by Degas fetched large prices. Forced to leave his home in the Rue Victor Massé, where he had lived for twenty years. Suzanne Valadon, who had become a close friend, found him a new studio and apartment at 6 Boulevard de Clichy, but he was never reconciled to the move.
1914	The Camondo collection, including magnificent works by Degas, entered the Louvre. This marked the complete victory of the Impressionists.
1917	Died on September 27th and was buried in the family vault in Montmartre cemetery.

SOME OBSERVATIONS ON ART BY DEGAS

Today, 18th January 1856, I had a great conversation with M. Soutzo. What courage there is in his studies. It is essential therefore never to bargain with nature. There is really courage in attacking nature frontally in her great planes and lines, and cowardice in doing it in details and facets. (From a note-book of 1856)

It seems to me that today, if the artist wishes to be serious — to cut out a little original niche for himself — or at least preserve his own innocence of personality — he must once more sink himself in solitude. There is too much talk and gossip; pictures are apparently made, like stockmarket prices, by the association of people eager for profit... All this traffic sharpens our intelligence and falsifies our judgment.
(Note-book of 1856)

What is certain is that to put a piece of nature in position and to draw it are two exceedingly different matters. (Note-book of 1863—7)

Seek to blend the spirit of Mantegna's armour with the animation and colour of Veronese. (Note-book of 1859—60)

How can one forget that the antique, the strongest art is also the most charming?
(Note-book of 1860, probably after visiting the Naples Museum)

Do portraits of people in familiar and typical attitudes; above all, give to their face the same choice of expression given to the body. So if it is typical of a person to laugh, make them laugh... of course, there are feelings which one can't render.
(Note-book of 1869)

After having done portraits seen from above, I will do some from below — sitting very close to a woman and looking at her from below I shall see her head glossy and surrounded with crystals. Do simple things, such as drawing a profile which does not move, moving oneself up or down, and the same for a whole body — a piece of furniture, a whole room. Do a series of arm movements in a dance or legs which do not move, turning oneself... Finally study a figure or an object, it does not matter which, from every viewpoint. One could use a mirror for that without changing one's position. Only the glass would be lowered or made to lean forward. One would turn round. Ideas for the studio. To put steps all round the room to get accustomed to drawing things from above and from below. Only paint things seen in the glass to get used to a hatred of *trompe l'oeil* effects.

For a portrait, set the pose on the ground floor and work on the first floor to get used to remembering forms and expressions and never draw or paint immediately.

Do a series of instruments and instrumentalists, their shapes, the twisting of a violinist's hands and arms and neck, for example, the swelling and hollowing cheeks of a bassoonist, etc.

Do a series in water-colour on mourning (different blacks), black veils of heavy mourning (floating over the face), black gloves, carriages in mourning, equipment of the company of funeral undertakers, carriages like Venetian gondoliers.

On smoke. Smoke of people smoking pipes, cigarettes, cigars, the smoke of trains, of high chimneys, of factories, of steamboats, etc. The crushing of smoke under bridges. Steam.

On evening. Infinite subjects. In the cafés, the different tones of the globes reflected in the glass.

On bakeries, bread, series on loaves, seen in the cellar or through the air-shafts of the road. Colours of rose flour — the beautiful curves of still lifes of different loaves, long, oval, fluted, round, etc. Essay in colour on the yellows, pinks, greys of loaves. Perspectives of piles of loaves. Delivery from bakeries. Cakes, wheat, mills, flour, sacks, strong men in the market. (Note-book of 1860—1)

There is a kind of shame in being known especially by people who do not understand you. A great reputation is therefore a sort of shame. (Note-book of 1878—84)

You know what I think of painters who work in the open. If I were the government I would have a company of police watching out for men who paint landscapes from nature. Oh, I don't wish for anybody's death; I should be quite content with a little buckshot to begin with... Renoir, that's different, he can do what he likes.
(Reported by many people, including André Gide, *Journal*, July 1909)

No art was ever less spontaneous than mine. What I do is the result of reflection and study of the great masters; of inspiration, spontaneity, temperament I know nothing.
(Reported by George Moore)

I have always tried to urge my colleagues to seek for new combinations along the path of draughtsmanship, which I consider a more fruitful field than that of colour. But they wouldn't listen to me and have gone the other way. (Said to Sickert in 1885)

A picture demands a certain mystery, vagueness, fantasy. If one dots all the i's, one ends by being boring. Even in front of nature, one must compose. There are people who believe that this is forbidden. Corot must have composed in front of nature, too. His charm derives above all from that. A picture is an original combination of lines and tones which make themselves felt...

(Criticising a picture of Jeanniot's) You have tried to render outside air, the air that one breathes, fresh air. Oh, well! a picture is first of all a product of the artist's imagination, it must never be a copy. If finally one can add two or three touches from nature, of course that won't do any harm. The air that one sees in the great masters' pictures is not the air one breathes.

It is all very well to copy what you see, but it is much better to draw only what you still see in your memory. This is a transformation in which imagination collaborates with memory. Then you only reproduce what has struck you, that is to say the essential, and so your memories and your fantasy are freed from the tyranny which nature holds over them. That is why pictures made in this way by a man who has cultivated his memory, knowing both the old masters and his craft well, are practically always remarkable. Look at Delacroix.
(Jeanniot: *Souvenirs sur Degas*, *Revue Universelle*, 1933)

If I were to enter the Luxembourg, I should believe I was being taken to the police-station. (Reported by Daniel Halévy)

One must treat the same subject ten times, even a hundred times. Nothing in art should seem to be accidental, not even movement.
(Letter to the sculptor Bartholomé, 1886)

Manet, more than I, would have seen beautiful things. He would not have made much of them though. We love and are inspired only by the familiar. The unfamiliar is in turn captivating and boring. (In a letter from New Orleans)

They call me the painter of dancers; they don't realise that for me the dancer has been a pretext for painting pretty materials and delineating movement.
Poor Manet! To have painted the *Maximilien*, the *Christ aux anges* and all the things he did before 1875 and to abandon his magnificient 'plum-juice' in order to paint linen.
(Vollard: *En écoutant Cézanne, Degas, Renoir*)

Nudes, until now, have always been depicted as the public likes to imagine them. But my women are simple, honest people whose only concern is the intimate business at hand... It's as if you were looking through a keyhole.
(Showing his pastels to George Moore; quoted by P. A. Lemoisne who knew Degas)

Painting is the art of surrounding a spot of Venetian red in such a way that it appears vermilion. (Quoted by P. A. Lemoisne)

We have lost everything when putting away our magician's hat. Now our secrets are scattered all over the streets... In the old days when speaking of a great artist, one thought Michel Angelo or Rembrandt. Now we know that it refers to a fashionable dressmaker! (Reported in the *Mémoires* of Elisabeth de Gramont, p. 115)

From time to time, I look at your drawing made in red pencil which is still hanging in the dining room, and I always tell myself 'This devilish Maria has a genius for drawing!'
(From a letter to Suzanne Valadon)

A painting is an artificial work existing outside nature, and it requires as much cunning as the perpetration of a crime.
(Quoted by Vuillard and others)

If I could have another twenty years time to work, I should do things that would endure. Am I to finish like that after racking my brains like one possessed and after having come so close to many methods of seeing and acting well? No. Remember the art of the Le Nain and all medieval France. Our race will have something simple and bold to offer. The naturalist movement will draw in a manner worthy of the great schools and then its strength will be recognised. This English art that appeals so much to us often seems to be exploiting some trick. We can do better than they and be just as strong... That fellow Whistler really has something in the sea- and water-pieces he showed me. But, bless me, there are quite different things to be done... I advise you to paint motifs of a varied nature and intensity. I think we are too fond of the demi-plein mince. (Degas' own expression, referring perhaps to thick technique; he himself laid on his colours very thinly at this time.)
(Letter to James Tissot, February 1873)

The realist movement no longer needs to fight with the others; it already *is*, it *exists*, it must show itself as *something distinct*, there must be a *salon of realists*. Manet does not understand that. I definitely think he is more vain than intelligent. So exhibit anything you like... Forget the money side for a moment. Exhibit. Be of your country and with your friends.
(Letter to Tissot, 1874, when Degas was organising the first Impressionist exhibition)

If I could have had my own way I would have confined myself entirely to black and white. But if one has the whole world on one's back, which wants colour and colour only! of all my work perhaps some drawings will remain.

We shall never know all the harm that chemistry has done to painting.

In our beginnings, Fantin, Whistler and I were all on the same road, the road from Holland. Go and see at the exhibition in the Quai Malaquais a small picture, a toilet scene by Fantin; we could have signed it, Whistler and I.
(Information communicated in Guérin's edition of Degas' letters by the lawyer Paul Poujaud)

I have a lot of trouble getting myself to work in the morning.

Cursed Monet! Everything he does is always immediately full of aplomb, while I give myself a lot of trouble and it isn't right!
(Reminiscences of Walter Sickert, Burlington Magazine, 1917)

NOTES ON THE PLATES
All works are in oil unless otherwise stated.

Plate 1 *Self-portrait with charcoal holder*, c. 1854—5. Musée du Louvre, Paris. 31⅞ × 26 in. (81 × 64.5 cm.). Degas drew and painted most of his self-portraits before he was twenty-five, when he was not yet a professional painter who could hire other models or receive commissions; his brothers and sisters, obliging as they seem to have been, cannot have been invariably free. Degas generally represented himself as serious, sometimes surly (in 1857 his friends the Tournys teased him about being a bear in company) with melancholy, questioning eyes. This work, probably executed in his father's house in the Rue de Mondivi, when Degas was just beginning to study with Lamothe, shows the soberness and firmness characteristic of his training in the school of Ingres. Only in the sixties did he paint self-portraits in the romantic tradition of Courbet and Delacroix, whom he had come to admire. A first sketch for this painting can be found in a note-book of 1854 presented by his family to the Bibliothèque Nationale.

Plate 2 *Portrait of René-Hilaire de Gas*, 1857. Musée du Louvre, Paris. 21⅝ × 16⅛ in. (55.25 × 41.25 cm.). The painter's grandfather was seventy-seven when this portrait was painted in his villa at Capodimonte, which was to be part of the painter's inheritance. René Hilaire de Gas had been a dealer in cereals in Paris at the time of the French Revolution, but had been forced to flee to Naples because his fiancée was one of the famous 'Young girls of Verdun', who had welcomed the Prussian army when it invaded France in 1792 to re-establish the monarchy. He became a banker and married an Italian girl; their ten children included Degas' father and Laure, who became Baroness Belleli. There are at least three studies for this portrait in a note-book of 1857, and next to them a copy of Titian's *Paul III* which Degas is thought to have used and reversed for this composition.

Plate 3 *The young Spartans*, 1860. National Gallery, London. 43½ × 61¼ in. (110.5 × 155.5 cm.). In later years Degas said that he had taken this subject from Plutarch; in the latter's life of Lycurgus, the lawgiver orders Spartan girls to wrestle with each other, but the idea of their inciting boys to fight is more likely to be derived from the Abbé Barthélemy's *Voyage du jeune Anarchis*, published in 1789, which was in Degas' school library. The composition probably owes something to Ingres' *Age d'or*; it may also be indebted to Chassériau's *Peace* — a decoration for the Cour des Comptes — and to Puvis de Chavannes' studies for *La Paix* in Amiens, both of which have a harmonious, lucid and heroic disposition of nudes similar to the Spartans, and both of which Degas probably knew. In a contemporary note-book Degas mentioned in connection with this a drawing in sanguine by Pontormo 'showing old women seated arguing and showing something'. There are many studies for this work in which one can watch Degas becoming more naturalistic and increasingly less interested in historical detail. It remained in his studio, and, like *The daughter of Jepthah* (plate 5) seems to have been worked on later.

Plate 4 *The Belleli family*, c. 1860—2. Musée du Louvre, Paris. 78¾ × 99⅝ in. (81 × 64.5 cm.). This original group-portrait, often considered the masterpiece of Degas' early career, was itself painted mainly in Paris on Degas' return from Italy, but he made numerous preparatory sketches in the Belleli's Florentine house and also painted two single portraits of his cousins' daughters in 1856, a double portrait in 1857 and another later still, in the early sixties. The importance of this picture for Degas can be measured by the fact that it probably kept this usually dutiful son from obeying his father's summons to return home, in the autumn of 1858. The baroness was his father's sister Laure, the baron was a Neapolitan friend and supporter of Cavour, exiled after the revolution of 1848 but later, after the establishment of the Kingdom of Italy in 1860, made a senator. The family were in mourning for a son, and the baroness had lost her father, Degas' grandfather, in 1858; at the time of the painting she was pregnant and Degas has given her a noble and unhappy expression. Unlike other nineteenth-century painters, such as Whistler and Fantin-Latour,

Degas has not shown any psychological relationship between the daughters; they are not sewing or playing the piano together, but, as in certain Renaissance works, are placed frontally, side by side, looking out of the picture. It has been suggested that Degas contrasted the prim, innocent-looking Giovanna, with the rather cocky, conscious indifference of her sister, her leg nonchalantly up on the chair, and also emphasised a lack of rapport between the wife and husband, who is withdrawn rather proudly, perhaps, from his family. The tonal organisation of the picture was developed in a preparatory pastel, which contrasts the black and white of mother and daughter with the light ground, and merges the baron with the middle grey to the right. Compositionally the picture is based on a series of rectangles against which play the curved figures; the fact that they turn inwards gives the work unity.

Plate 5 *The daughter of Jepthah*, c. 1861–4. Smith College Museum of Art, Northampton, Massachusetts. 30¼ × 46 in. (77 × 117 cm.). One of the largest, most complex and least economical in effect of all Degas' works. He was much engrossed in planning it during 1859–61 (see Introduction, p. 10) and filled his *carnets* with sketches, notes about colour, ways of expressing the movement and relationship of Jepthah's daughter and her companions (at the back) to the landscape. Degas' new admiration for Delacroix, particularly the *Justice of Trajan*, which he copied, is apparent in the position of Jepthah and his unlikely looking horse, but the figures are firmly planted in their place; Degas has either not attempted or not achieved the rhythmical evidence of Delacroix.

Jepthah, a judge of Israel, before fighting a battle with the Ammonites, vowed to make a burnt offering of the first thing which came from his house on his return. He was met by his daughter and her maidens and 'did unto her his vow'.

Plate 6 *Princess Pauline de Metternich*, c. 1861–71. National Gallery, London. 16 × 11½ in. (40 × 29 cm.). This rather strange and delicate portrait of the wife of the Austro-Hungarian ambassador at Napoleon III's court, was discovered in 1937 to be copied partly from a *carte de visite* photograph by Disderi, taken in 1860. In the photograph, she is standing in a crinoline, with her left arm in that of the prince, her husband, whom Degas has suppressed, together with the arm. It is difficult to date (Aron Scharf, in his dissertation on the influence of photography, considers it in the early sixties, and the National Gallery catalogue in the seventies), but between 1865 and 1870, Degas made about fifty portraits, often very subtle in their rendering of facial structure and character.

Plate 7 *Portrait of Léon Bonnat*, c. 1863. Musée Bonnat, Bayonne. 16⅞ × 14⅛ in. (43 × 36 cm.). Léon Joseph Florentin Bonnat (1833–1922), later a fashionable portrait-painter and benefactor of Bayonne, studied in Madrid and Paris, where he probably met Degas about 1855 at the Ecole des Beaux-Arts. He won the second Grand Prix de Rome and went to Italy in 1858, where he became a member of the same small group as Degas. He first became known for his picture *Adam and Eve finding the body of Abel* (1860) and then painted many Italian genre pictures, religious subjects and, above all, portraits including those of Hugo, Pasteur, Thiers, Dumas and Renan. Although Manet and his friends at the Café Guerbois naturally did not approve of his orthodoxy, Degas himself always liked him and corrected himself after making an acid remark about Bonnat's painting to Halévy, saying, 'No, he is nice and an old friend.' Of this portrait, with its formal hat and black eyes, Degas used to say that Bonnat looked like a Venetian ambassador.

Plate 8 *Scene of war in the Middle Ages* or *The disasters befalling the city of Orleans*, 1865. Musée du Louvre, Paris. 32⅝ × 45 in. (83 × 145 cm.). This, the last of Degas' history pictures, was exhibited at the Salon of 1865 and praised by Puvis de Chavannes. It has more movement than the *Spartans* and *Sémiramis* and shows the influence of Moreau and Delacroix, who also liked to depict tortured women. Degas' copy of Delacroix's *Battle of Poitiers* may have suggested the subject, and Orleans was perhaps chosen because the Degas family had links with this city, rather than because of any specific incident in history. This picture has also been associated with Moreau's and Degas' enthusiasm for the works of the Flemish Hans Memling (died 1494), but the latter generally painted calmer subjects. There are about twenty preparatory drawings for this in the Louvre and others in the note-books.

Plate 9 *The meet*, c. 1864–8. Private Collection, Basle. 27½ × 35 in. (70 × 89 cm.). French taste for English sports increased considerably during the reign of Louis-Philippe (even earlier, in 1822, Géricault had painted *Epsom Derby* and Carl Vernet then produced many racing pictures). During the late fifties, Degas had painted horses on his travels, and he used rather archaic or wooden-looking animals, sometimes inspired by *quattrocento* models, for his history pictures (see plates 5 and 8). But after visiting the Valpinçons in Normandy (*c.* 1860—1), he became more interested in racing and the movement of horses, although at first he found it difficult to draw them convincingly (in early years, he was often a careful and deliberate, rather than a brilliant or facile, draughtsman). Here, he is more successful in the contrived spontaneity of his grouping than in detailed naturalism. Muybridge's photographs of horses in action, later so much used by Degas, were probably not available until the eighties.

Plate 10 *The woman with chrysanthemums*, 1865. Metropolitan Museum of Art, New York. 29 × 36½ in. (73 × 92 cm.). This signed and dated picture is probably the first example of decentralised composition in Degas' work which, carried so far, seemed strange to many contemporaries. It was painted in oil thinned with turpentine and mounted on canvas. The wonderful colours of the flowers and the blue-grey dress serve to demonstrate that Degas' mastery of colour was not confined to his later years but appeared as soon as the influence of Delacroix, Moreau and the Venetians helped to emancipate him from the school of Ingres.

Plate 11 *The orchestra of the Paris Opéra*, 1868. Musée du Louvre, Paris. 20⅞ × 17¾ in. (53 × 45 cm.). This is partly a group portrait, partly an attempt to use musical instruments as a decorative theme, an idea foreshadowed in Degas' note-books, which also contain sketches of harps, pianos, violinists, etc. From left to right the composer Emmanuel Chabrier, then Pagans; Pillet, cellist; Gard, stage director of the ballets; Piot-Normand, painter; the composer Souquet; Doctor Pillot; Désiré Dihau, bassoonist; Altès, flautist; Laucien, first violinist; Gouffé, bassist. In 1870 Degas gave this picture, which he considered unfinished, to Désiré Dihau, who had virtually introduced him into the world of the orchestra. Degas' family, who disliked his constant retouching of works, told Dihau that thanks to his having kept the picture away from the painter, a finished work had been achieved.

Plate 12 *Mme Camus at the piano*, 1869. Bührle Collection, Zürich. 54¾ × 37 in. (139 × 94 cm.). This picture, which was refused at the Salon of 1869 although another of Degas' portraits was accepted, shows the wife of Dr Camus, a friend of both Manet and Degas who was interested in Japanoiserie. There are at least five studies for it including a careful sketch of her arm, and one of the contents of the room, piano, cushion, etc. In the final picture these are treated with an exact, almost Dutch fidelity, which makes the Salon's refusal surprising. Except for the sitter's position, the work is not particularly startling — another portrait of Mme Camus has a much more unusual theme in its treatment of firelight. In these years immediately before Degas' pre-occupation with ballet, he painted a great number of musicians, including Mlle Dihau at the piano, the violinist Pillet and various studies of orchestras and singers.

Plate 13 *Portrait of Hortense Valpinçon as a child*, *c.* 1869. Minneapolis Institute of Arts. 29 × 43⅛ in. (73.5 × 109.2 cm.). The Valpinçons were relations of the collector who owned the *Odalisque* of Ingres. Degas often visited them in Normandy, and it may have been there that he painted their child in a typically life-like position of arrested movement, holding a half-eaten apple. Degas was unsentimental about children, but he liked them and often drew them. His note-books show that he often allowed children to draw in them. Daniel Halévy recorded Degas' kindness to him when he was a boy. Later, Degas modelled a large bust of Hortense, but it was damaged and no longer exists.

Plate 14 *Degas' father listening to Pagans*, c. 1869—72. Musée du Louvre, Paris. 31½ × 24¾ in. (80 × 63 cm.). Lorenzo Pagans, a celebrated Spanish singer, often took part in musical evenings at the homes of Degas and Manet. The canvas is divided in an unusual way by the vertical of the guitar, and the colour is restricted mainly to tans, browns, grey and white. The intelligent, reflective face of Degas' father shown against the sheet of music, reminds one that his letters to Edgar show him to be a most perceptive and encouraging critic of his son's early work, and that not all prosperous bankers would have acquiesced so readily in their eldest son's abandonment of law for painting.

Plate 15 *Mlle Dobigny*, 1869. Private Collection, Zürich. 12¼ × 10⅛ in. (31 × 26 cm.). This signed and dated portrait shows the model who posed for Corot, Henri Rouart and for the picture *Hope* by Puvis de Chavannes.

Plate 16 *Mlle Marie Dihau*, c. 1869—1872. Musée du Louvre, Paris. 8¾ × 10½ in. (22 × 27 cm.). Another of Degas' pictures of musicians. Mlle Dihau, the sister of Degas' friend Désiré, the bassoonist, is called 'my cruel friend' in one of Degas' letters to his brother, and this has led to suggestions that Degas was once in love with her. Mlle Dihau owned this and another portrait of her, now in the Metropolitan Museum, New York, which was painted in a restaurant ('Chez la mère Lefebvre' frequented by Degas and the Dihaus) in order to console her for having to go away to Lille, where she then lived. Mlle Dihau was also a fine singer; she gave concerts and appeared in Berlioz' opera *Beatrice et Benedict*.

Plate 17 *The woman at the window*, c. 1871–2. Courtauld Gallery, London. 24¼ × 18¼ in. (62 × 46.5 cm.). There is uncertainty about the date of this picture, but Sickert quotes Degas as saying that it was painted 'during or soon after the seige', i.e. 1871–2. Certainly this is about the time that both in his notes and in his pictures (e.g. *Mme Camus in red*) Degas was interested in strange experiments with light. The picture is unfinished, and the medium is *essence* (petrol), not oil. The identity of the sitter is not known.

Plate 18 *The woman with the vase of flowers*, 1872. Musée du Louvre, Paris. 25¾ × 21¼ in. (65 × 54 cm.). Signed and dated, this portrait was painted by Degas when he visited his brother René in New Orleans, and shows the latter's wife, who married him after her first husband was killed in the Civil War. She was born Estelle Musson, a cousin of the Degas family and was, at this time, blind, though Degas' letters describe her moving about the house without clumsiness, as if she could see. Later on, René left her and married again, and this so angered his brother Edgar that for many years he would not see him. Degas' letters from New Orleans showed that he admired Estelle's courage and that their home life suggested to him that he might still marry.

Plate 19 *Mrs William Bell* or *Mme René de Gas*. 1872–3. National Gallery of Art, Washington, D.C. (Chester Dale Collection). 28¾ × 36¼ in. (73 × 92 cm.). Also painted in New Orleans. Lemoisne had identified the sitter as Mrs Bell, born Mathilde Musson, and Degas' cousin, the elder sister of his brother's wife. However, a note in the National Gallery (Washington, D.C.) catalogue states that 'she is more generally identified as Mathilde's sister Estelle, wife of the artist's brother René. The fixed expression of the eyes lends support to the latter identification, since Estelle had been blind for several years when this portrait was painted...' In any case, the painting of her delicate muslin dress shows great subtlety and assurance.

Plate 20 *The cotton market, New Orleans*, 1873. Musée de Pau, France. 29⅛ × 36¼ in. (74 × 92 cm.). This was one of the first of Degas' works to enter a museum; it was purchased by the city of Pau in 1878. It is perhaps the most perfect example of naturalism in all nineteenth-century painting. Degas' brother René, whom he visited in New Orleans (1872–3), was in the cotton business, and he is shown here in the centre reading a newspaper; his father-in-law Michel Musson is the elderly gentleman in the foreground, testing a sample of cotton. As usual, the casual-looking arrangement is deceptive, and the figures, made from preparatory drawings, are carefully organised and interwoven. Notice the skilful use of limited colours — the repetition of black and white against the cool green and tan. This picture has had many detractors. René Huyghe describes it thus: '... the materialism of the mercantile *bourgeoisie* surprised in its inner sanctum and depicted at its source; this snapshot reveals unadulterated triviality.' Others have assumed that Degas only painted it to oblige his brother.

Plate 21 *The pedicure*, 1873. Musée du Louvre, Paris (Collection Camondo). 24 × 18⅛ in. (61 × 46 cm.). This picture was probably painted soon after Degas' return to Paris from drafts and sketches made in New Orleans. The young girl seen in the painting was probably Joe Balfour, his brother René's step-daughter, by Estelle Musson *(The woman with the flowerpot)* who had previously been married and lost her husband in the American Civil War. Although the subject is really more startling than that of *Absinthe* (plate 28), its sober simplicity, the light colours and almost idyllic nursery atmosphere perhaps rendered it less objectionable. It is both an excellent example of Degas' capacity to seize the crucial and revealing moment like a camera, and a prelude to the bathroom scenes of nearly twenty years later.

Plate 22 *The dance foyer at the Opéra, Rue le Peletier*, 1872. Musée du Louvre, Paris (Camondo Collection). 12½ × 18⅛ in. (32 × 46 cm.). This shows the ballet-master Moraine teaching some of his students. The Rue le Peletier is probably specified here because in the autumn of 1873 this opera house was destroyed by fire and Garnier's New Opera House was not opened until 1875. (Meanwhile performances and rehearsals of ballet were held in the Salle Ventadour which Degas painted.) Although the dancers are individualised, Degas has woven them together in an ensemble with a characteristic use of empty space and concern for the organisation of the picture as a whole. Another small work with the same title, painted the same year, but entirely different in composition was bought by Degas' friend Mary Cassatt for an American collector and is now in the Metropolitan Museum, New York. Miss Lilian Browse has pointed out in her *Degas dancers* that although the painter certainly knew the correct practice-costumes of the day, he sometimes, as here, added velvet sashes and bows for decorative effect, although the dancers did not have them. This is, of course, characteristic of his creed 'Even in front of nature one must compose'.

Plate 23 *Carriage at the races*, c. 1870–3. Museum of Fine Arts, Boston. 14$\frac{1}{8}$ × 21$\frac{5}{8}$ in. (36 × 55 cm.). This picture, like so many of the more delicately coloured works by Degas, is impossible to judge from reproductions. In the original it is a cool, subtle balance of greyish greens and blacks that recall Corot rather than Degas' Impressionist friends. The way in which the victoria is placed in the bottom corner of the canvas and cut sharply may have been influenced by Degas' interest both in photography and Japanese prints, although it must be remembered that some masters of antiquity and of the Renaissance had already used much the same device. Degas himself said that the landscape in Normandy, where he went to the races, reminded him of England, and here the carriage, the driver's top hat and the bulldog show the French taste for English fashions at this time. Degas had been on a visit to London with Manet in 1868 and passed through on his way to the United States in 1872.

Plate 24 *Head of a woman*, c. 1873. Tate Gallery, London. 6$\frac{3}{4}$ × 7$\frac{3}{4}$ in. (17.5 × 20 cm.). Like so many other works, this sketch was still in Degas' studio when he died. It probably belonged afterwards to his friend Paul Lafond, who wrote perceptively about Degas' life and work. In the sixties and seventies, Degas was much occupied with the subtle rendering of human character, both in portrait and genre; in this, he was one of the few major artists of his generation which was, of course, intensely preoccupied with light and landscape.

Plate 25 *Interior (The Rape)*, c. 1874. Collection of Henry P. McIlhenny, Philadelphia. 32 × 45$\frac{1}{2}$ in. (81 × 116 cm.). In a few genre pictures of the seventies, Degas came near to telling stories of contemporary life in the manner of Duranty or the Goncourts. It has been suggested that this picture illustrates an incident in Duranty's novel *Les Combats de Françoise Duquesnoy*, but more plausible perhaps is Jean Adhémar's explanation: in Zola's *Madeleine Ferat*, the newly married couple arrive at a hotel and Madeleine weeps, saying, 'You suffer, for you love me, and I cannot be yours.' But if the man embodies 'stupor and brutality', as some critics declare, the first source is more probable. Notice how Degas has separated the two characters by almost the whole space of the room, and how the prettiness of the wallpaper and touches of white give additional pathos to the kneeling girl. Owing to an accident, this painting had to be repaired and retouched in the years 1900 to 1905; Degas did this with the help of the Italian painter Chialiva.

Plate 26 *Reherseal of a ballet on the stage*, 1874. Musée du Louvre, Paris (Camondo Collection). 26 × 32$\frac{1}{4}$ in. (66 × 82 cm.). This monochrome work was shown at the first Impressionist exhibition in 1874. There is another picture of the same title and very similar composition in the Metropolitan Museum, New York. It is characteristic of Degas, and perhaps of the modern sensibility, which he did much to shape, that one can accept simultaneously in his picture the glamourised light and delicate dresses together with a dancer scratching her back, as if unobserved, and others yawning and stretching. As usual, Degas has made skilful use of a large empty space at the front of the stage.

Plate 27 *Pouting*, c. 1874–6. The Metropolitan Museum of Art, New York. 12$\frac{3}{4}$ × 18$\frac{1}{4}$ in. (32 × 46 cm.). This picture was probably also called 'The Banker', and if so Degas was dissatisfied with it and asked Fauré, the singer, to buy it back from Durand-Ruel for him. In 1885, certainly, he started to do a big sketch of another version. It has generally been assumed that the girl is the man's daughter or young wife who is waiting for his attack of sulks to die down before she shows him some note or bill. The life-like appearance of the room is probably due to the fact that the picture was based on a photograph taken by Degas himself, for which he made Madame Arthur Fontaine and his friend the lawyer M. Poujaud pose. The photograph still exists and shows that Degas followed its composition closely.

Plate 28 *Absinthe*, 1876. Musée du Louvre, Paris. 36$\frac{1}{4}$ × 26$\frac{3}{4}$ in. (92 × 68.5 cm.). For this picture Degas posed two of his friends, the engraver Marcellin Desboutin and the actress Ellen Andrée, on the terrace of the Nouvelle-Athènes Café in the Place Pigalle, which after the Franco-Prussian War was the new rendezvous of the artists, later to be called Impressionists, who had met before in the Café Guerbois. Shown in London in 1893, it caused a scandal and the owner sold it, although George Moore and Walter Sickert came to its defence. Degas was in his forties, too mature and sophisticated to be fascinated by vice in the same way as later the young Toulouse-Lautrec and Picasso were attracted to it. The theme is treated coolly and objectively and the main interest seems reserved for the zig-zagging lines which begin at the bottom of the canvas and the off-centre position of the figures, one of which is cut by the frame. This kind of design may owe something to Degas' study of Japanese prints.

Plate 29 *Mlle Malo, c.* 1877. The Barber Institute of Fine Arts, Birmingham. Pastel, $20\frac{5}{8} \times 15\frac{3}{4}$ in. (52×41 cm.). One of four studies Degas made of Mlle Malo, a dancer at the Paris Opéra; this pastel belonged to the painter Jacques-Emil Blanche. Degas' portraits are always saved from any commonplace fixity of expression partly by his habit, which he learnt from the Italian old masters, of not carrying the delineation of the sitter's mouth too far. He wrote of the *Mona Lisa* that the most remarkable thing about it was its power of non-expression. (The note-book here is difficult to read, and he may have written 'expression'.)

Plate 30 *Café-concert at the Ambassadeurs, c.* 1876–7. Musée de Lyons, France. Pastel, $14\frac{1}{2} \times 10\frac{5}{8}$ in. (37×27 cm.). This picture began with a monotype, a painting on a metal plate which Degas drew and then transferred to paper. As so often, Degas has depicted the contrast between the brilliant lighting of the stage and the more softly illuminated auditorium. At first, the audience may appear a confused jumble, but notice how the eye is led to the main singer on the stage by the top of the bass viol and her bright red dress, how the blue dress of another performer is echoed by the blue hat in the audience, and how the rectangle of pillars on the stage is repeated by the rectangle of the orchestra pit.

Plate 31 *At the sea-side: little girl having her hair combed by her nurse, c.* 1876–7. National Gallery, London (Lane Bequest). $18\frac{1}{2} \times 32\frac{1}{2}$ in. (47×82.5 cm.). This picture is painted on paper with oil thinned with turpentine and was exhibited in the third Impressionist Exhibition of 1877. It is sometimes said to be influenced by works of Manet, and Boudin, whom Degas knew, is also a possible source, but the characteristic and beautiful relation of empty space to the figures, and the witty organisation of objects such as the cap, bathing dress and umbrella are very much Degas' own. Vollard claimed that Degas said it was painted in the studio, not in the open air, and although the picture-dealer's reminiscences are not always reliable, this is true of some of Degas' landscapes and backgrounds.

Plate 32 *Women at a café: evening, c.* 1877. Musée du Louvre, Paris. Pastel on monotype, $16 \times 25\frac{5}{8}$ in. (41×65 cm.). This picture, exhibited at the third Impressionist exhibition in 1877 probably represents prostitutes outside a café on the Boulevard Montmartre, becoming bored and quarrelsome (one is biting her thumb contemptuously at another). Degas also made studies of women inside brothels, and, according to the Goncourt brothers, his interest in them was not limited to painting. Notice the almost classical construction of the picture by means of vertical lines and the masterly use of delicate pastel over monotype. Degas' colours here seem to foreshadow Vuillard, and this pastel was chosen in a recent French exhibition of the Nabis to exemplify Degas' influence on the group.

Plate 33 *Dancer bowing with a bouquet, c.* 1877. Musée du Louvre, Paris (Collection Camondo). Pastel, $29\frac{1}{2} \times 30\frac{3}{4}$ in. (75×78 cm.). There are at least eight paintings of a ballerina bowing with or without a bouquet, and they were all painted at roughly the same period. It is not certain which work is here being performed, but attempts have been made to identify it with *L'Africaine* by Meyerbeer or Chéret's décor for Massenet's *Le Roi de Lahore*. All the ballets of this time were performed in appropriate costumes, not in the simple ballet skirts which Degas has chosen to retain in a typical disregard for factual realism. The yellow sunshades behind the curtseying dancer are a particularly brilliant feature of this work.

Plate 34 *The rehearsal, c.* 1877. Glasgow Art Gallery (Burrell Collection). 23×33 in. (66×100 cm.). Like all Degas' pictures, this was not painted on the spot but in his studio where he had a spiral staircase and kept a collection of ballet frocks, shoes and sashes, etc. The models were girls actually training at the opera. Notice how Degas has used strong colours for the foreground figures and delicate yellows and pinks for those dancing by the window. A preparatory drawing for this picture shows that Degas was still using a plumb line, and that he had planned the exact position of the figures even down to their skirts. We are reminded that he praised Puvis de Chavannes, saying that no one else had so well found the exact place for each figure in his pictures, so that it was impossible to move any of them without spoiling the whole.

Plate 35 *Edmond Duranty*, 1879. Glasgow Art Gallery (Burrell Collection). Distemper, water-colour and pastel. 39½ × 39½ in. (100 × 100 cm.). Louis Emile Edmond Duranty (1833–80) critic and novelist, had been a disciple of Courbet's friend Champfleury, but he was less Socialist and humanitarian, more interested in an exact observation of contemporary town life than was the group around Courbet. Degas met him among Manet's friends in the Café Guerbois, and the artist and novelist greatly influenced each other's work. Duranty edited a periodical *Le Réalisme* (c. 1857) and later, in 1876, he published a brochure, *La Nouvelle Peinture*, which was in effect if not in intention a perceptive defence of those later called Impressionists, many of whom were his friends. He introduced Degas under his real name into his novel *Le Peintre Louis Martin*. The original use of Duranty's books in this composition may have suggested Cézanne's somewhat similar background to his portrait of Gustave Geoffroy. There is a preliminary smaller version in pastel and various studies of Duranty's head and bookshelves.

Plate 36 *Miss Lola at the Cirque Fernando*, 1879. National Gallery, London. 46¼ × 30½ in. (117.5 × 77.5 cm.). Degas' taste for showing movement at a crucial point naturally drew him to the circus, and it has also been suggested that in depicting the hard-won, disciplined skill of an acrobat or ballet-dancer he was symbolising his own stern struggle for perfection. Miss Lola is being drawn up to the roof by means of a rope held between her teeth; the girders of the roof repeat the angles of her limbs. There are several preparatory drawings for this work, which Degas seems to have done after getting to know the acrobat privately. This circus was the subject of several pictures painted by Toulouse-Lautrec (c. 1888) who admired Degas immensely.

Plate 37 *Miss Cassatt at the Louvre*, 1880. Collection of Henry P. McIlhenny, Philadelphia. Pastel. 23½ × 18½ in. (60 × 47 cm.). There are three pastels besides the etching of this subject; this is a study for the larger work showing the gallery. Degas' close friendship with Mary Cassatt (see Introduction) is illustrated by the fact that when he prepared his own list of contributors to the fourth exhibition of the Impressionists, he also made a list in one of his note books of Miss Cassatt's eleven works for the same show. Nevertheless he told a friend that in these studies he wished to show woman's crushed respect and absence of all feeling in the presence of art.

Plate 38 *Jockeys in the rain*, c. 1881. Glasgow Art Gallery (Burrell Collection). Pastel, 18½ × 25 in. (47 × 65 cm.). This picture is based in part on drawings made much earlier (c. 1866–72). Although it is not a study of violent movement like some of the race-course scenes, the relationship of the various horses to each other and to the surrounding space is very skilfully worked out and reminds one of the painter's classical training and tastes.

Plate 39 *Woman putting on her corset*, c. 1883. Musée des Beaux-Arts, Algiers. Pastel, 24¾ × 20¾ in. (63 × 52 cm.). This subject would have satisfied Degas' liking for the tense movements of bodies and for actions which have usually gone unperceived by onlookers. In a note-book, probably c. 1878–84, Degas reminds himself to study various objects showing their human use, and he includes corsets which have just been taken off and still bear the shape of the figure.

Plate 40 *Bed-time*, c. 1883. Tate Gallery, London. Pastel on monotype, 9 × 17½ in. (23 × 44.5 cm.). This small pastel appears to show the effect of Degas' growing interest in sculpture and the exploration of mass. The pastel was done over a second pull of one of Degas' monotypes. Denis Rouart writes that he sometimes took a second or even third pull of his prints, which were then very pale, and used them as points of departure for works which might be much changed and elaborated. Ronald Alley, in the Tate Gallery catalogue, points out that he has here changed a night-time scene, lit from a single source, into day-time. The delicate, subdued colours may be contrasted with the evidence of some later pastels.

Plate 41 *Two laundresses*, c. 1884. Musée du Louvre, Paris. 29⅞ × 32¼ in. (79 × 73 cm.). This is one of three variants on the same composition. Laundresses were a favourite subject of Degas in the eighties, but unlike Daumier he was not interested particularly in the pathos of these women and their poverty, but in their rhythmical muscular action, which he could probably see through shop windows during his innumerable walks through Paris. The bottle held by one of the women is probably not wine, as has been suggested, but water for sprinkling. Picasso made several well-known versions of the same subject, but his women have a Gothic or 'mannerist' slenderness with prominent shoulders.

Plate 42 *The tub*, 1886. Musée du Louvre, Paris. Pastel on cardboard, 23⅝ × 32⅝ in. (61 × 85 cm.). This was one of the series exhibited in the eighth Impressionist exhibition (1886). The characteristic view from above of a body straining in purposeful movement was described by Huysmans as a red-haired, corpulent, swollen female, and he goes on to write of 'this unique emphasis on the hateful or the contemptible', but also admits the artist's unforgettable veracity and the lucid, controlled drawing produced in a sort of cold fever, and defends Degas from the charge of obscenity ('Never have works been so lacking in slyness or questionable overtones... They even glorify a carnal disdain as never since the Middle Ages has an artist dared to do.'). That such works were generally considered ugly shows to what an extent the public were conditioned to the slippery or vaporous idealisations of the academies. This type of picture by Degas exerted a great effect on Bonnard and Vuillard and, probably, on Picasso's early *Blue Room*.

Plate 43 *The millinery shop*, c. 1884. Art Institute of Chicago. Pastel, 39½ × 43¼ in. (100 × 111 cm.). Of the subjects which Degas treated continuously in series, the hatshops are among the last to appear, towards 1876. He was particularly attracted by the delicate play of hands against the brilliant and sumptuous materials. This pastel was shown in the eighth Impressionist exhibition in 1886, and once belonged to Degas' friend Alexis Rouart. Degas often accompanied his woman friends to the milliners and dress-makers. Once he was sitting so raptly that his friend asked him what was so interesting. He replied, 'The red hands of the young girl holding the pins.'

Plate 44 *At the Tuileries: the woman with the umbrella*, c. 1887–90. Glasgow Art Gallery (Burrell Collection). 10⅝ × 7⅞ in. (27 × 20 cm.). It will be seen here that Degas did sometimes use oil in his later years, but generally for small works like this, which would not try his failing eyesight for too long. This is very freely painted with broad brushstrokes in comparison with the meticulous smoothness of his early oil technique.

Plate 45 *The morning toilet*, 1886. Metropolitan Museum of Art, New York. Pastel, 28¾ × 23¼ in. (73 × 59 cm.). This was also one of the series exhibited at the eighth Impressionist exhibition, but unlike most of the others it is calm and monumental, and hair dressing is not represented as a bodily struggle. The statuesque beauty of the sitter against the splendid and subtle colours of the sofa and maid's dress is remarkable, and give the lie to those critics who accused Degas of contemptuous misogyny. Douglas Cooper suggests that this nude is slightly reminiscent of works by Manet and Renoir and of a sculpture Degas did about the same time — *A dancer resting, hands on her haunches.*

Plate 46 *Woman combing her hair*, c. 1887–90. Musée du Louvre, Paris. Pastel, 32¼ × 22½ in. (82 × 57 cm.). This is a good example of Degas' later pastel studies of the nude which are treated very broadly and freely in sharp acid colours.

Plate 47 *Combing the hair*, c. 1892–5. National Gallery, London. 45 × 57½ in. (114 × 146 cm.). This work, which is unfinished, is difficult to date, as are many other of Degas' later works. It is probably a re-working of a pastel executed about 1885, or it could possibly be an earlier version of this pastel. There are at least two other sketches connected with it. The straining position of the seated women in contrast with the calm stance of the maid is characteristic of Degas' many treatments of this subject. This picture was once in the collection of Henri Matisse.

Plate 48 *Russian dancer*, 1895. Cummings Collection, Chicago. Pastel, 26⅜ × 22½ in. (67 × 57 cm.). In 1895 a troupe of Russian dancers were performing in national costume at the Folies Bergère, and Degas made about twenty drawings and pastels of them, all in very warm colours. The best known (e.g. *Russian dancers* in Stockholm) show three dancers together. In this sketch the movement of the skirt is more particularised than that of the body. It has been suggested that the Russian dancers were those of Diaghilev's ballet, but as Douglas Cooper points out, when this company first came to Paris in 1909 Degas was no longer capable of this kind of work. His last works are very large pastels and charcoal drawings, portraits of his friends the Rouarts and large, strongly coloured dancers, which he kept in his studio; he probably would not have approved their public exhibition. Lemoisne writes that he went on working until the very last year of his life, but his increasing blindness made it difficult to complete many rough drafts.

1

2

3

4

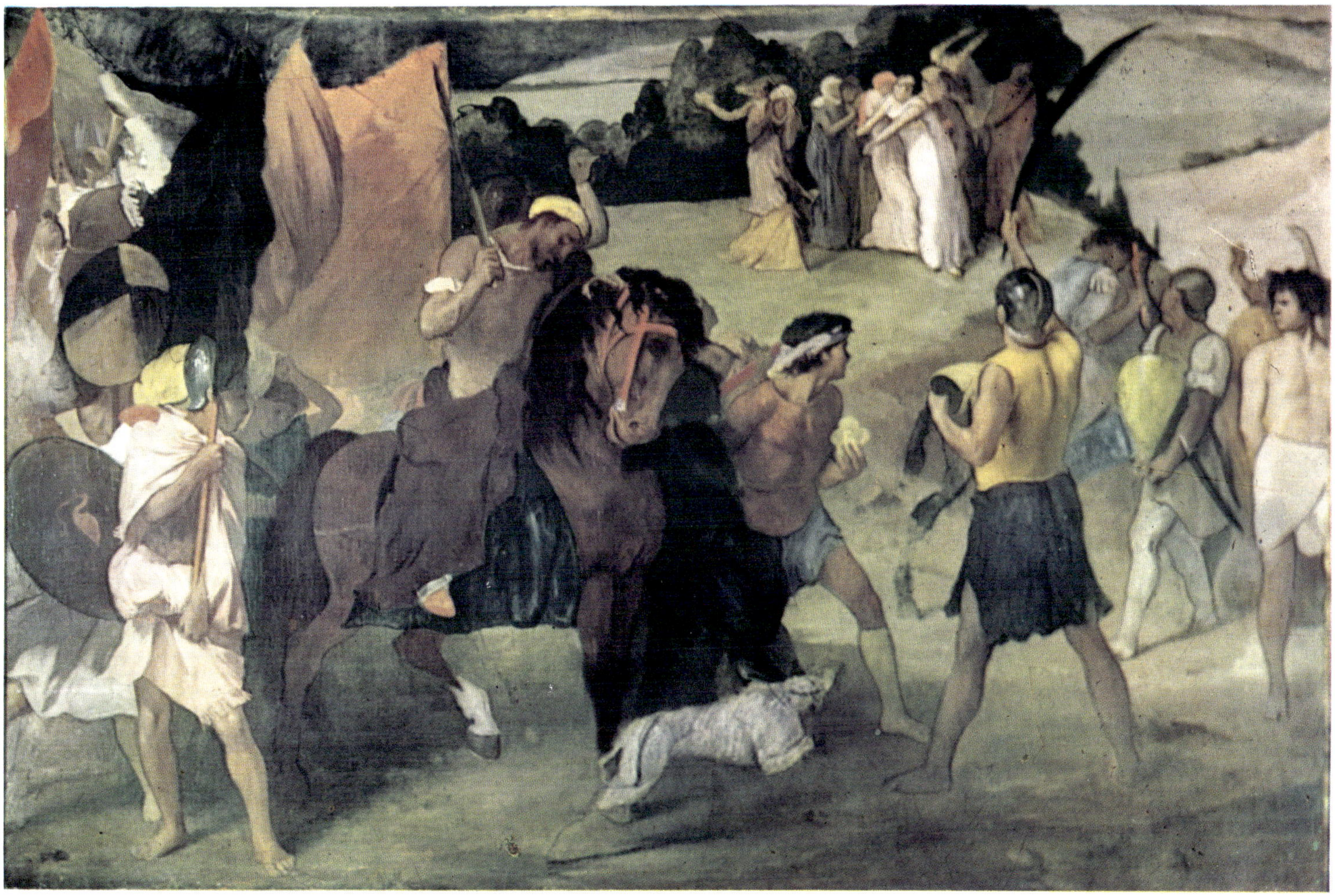

5

6

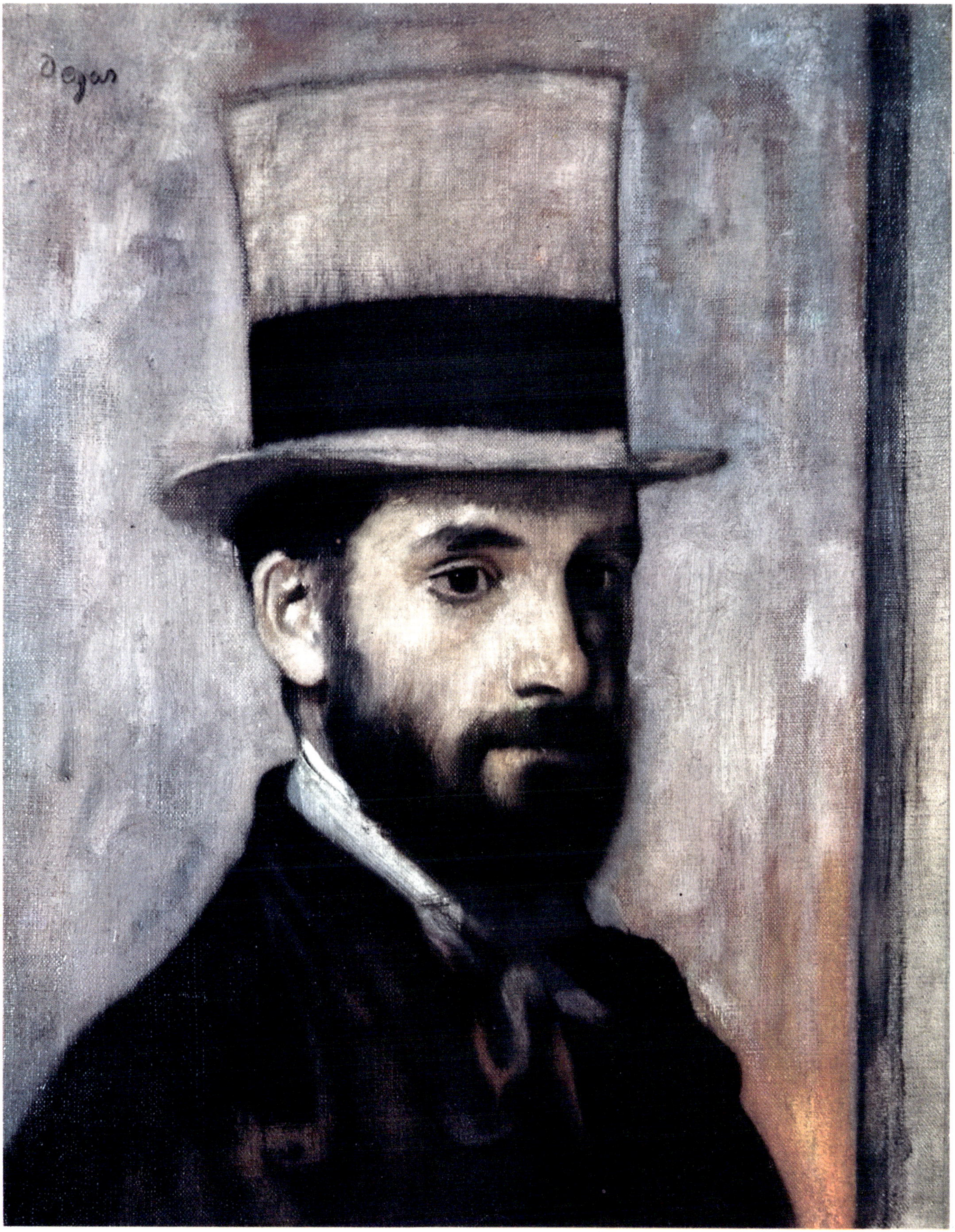
Degas

8

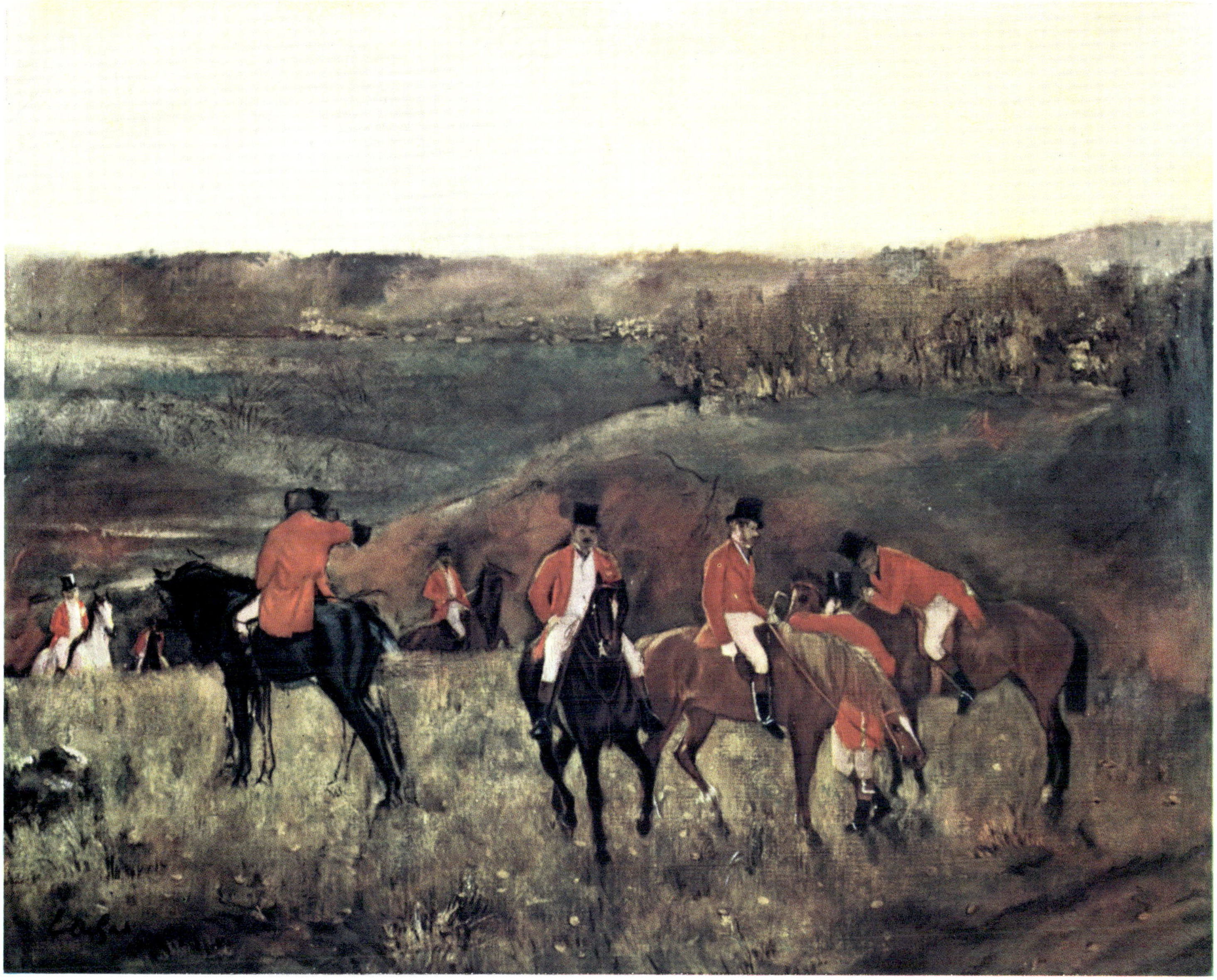

10

11

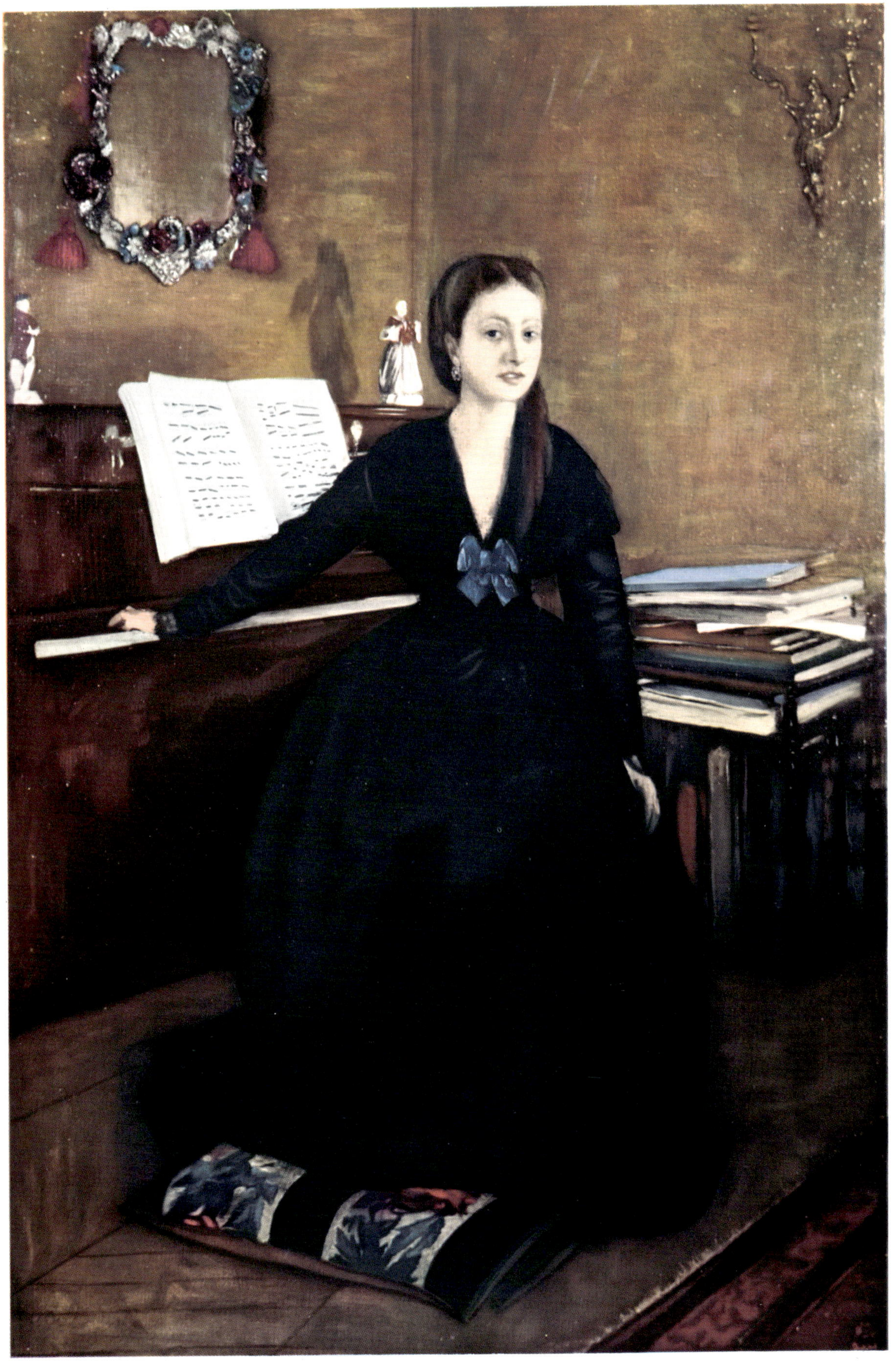

13

14

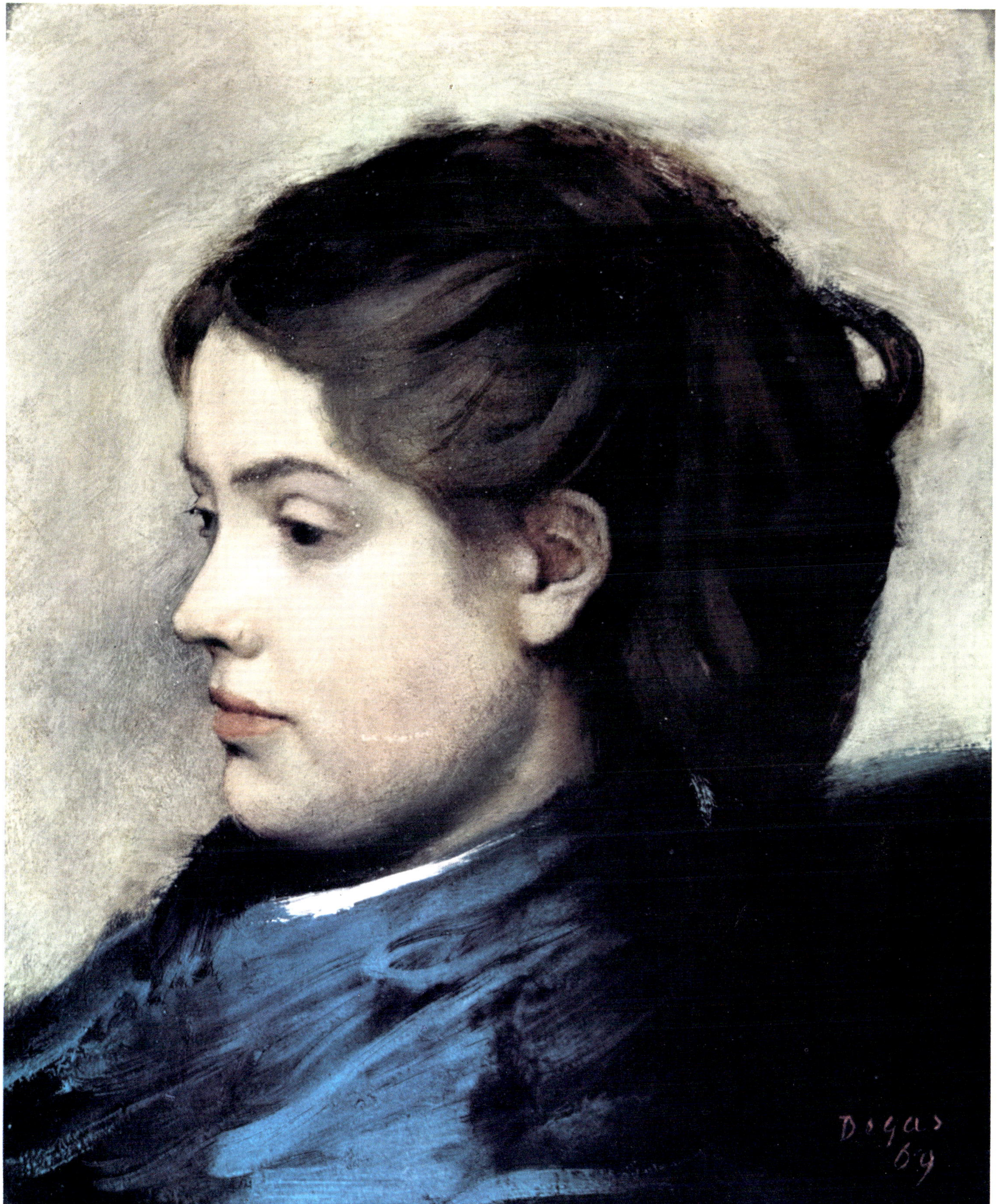
Degas
69

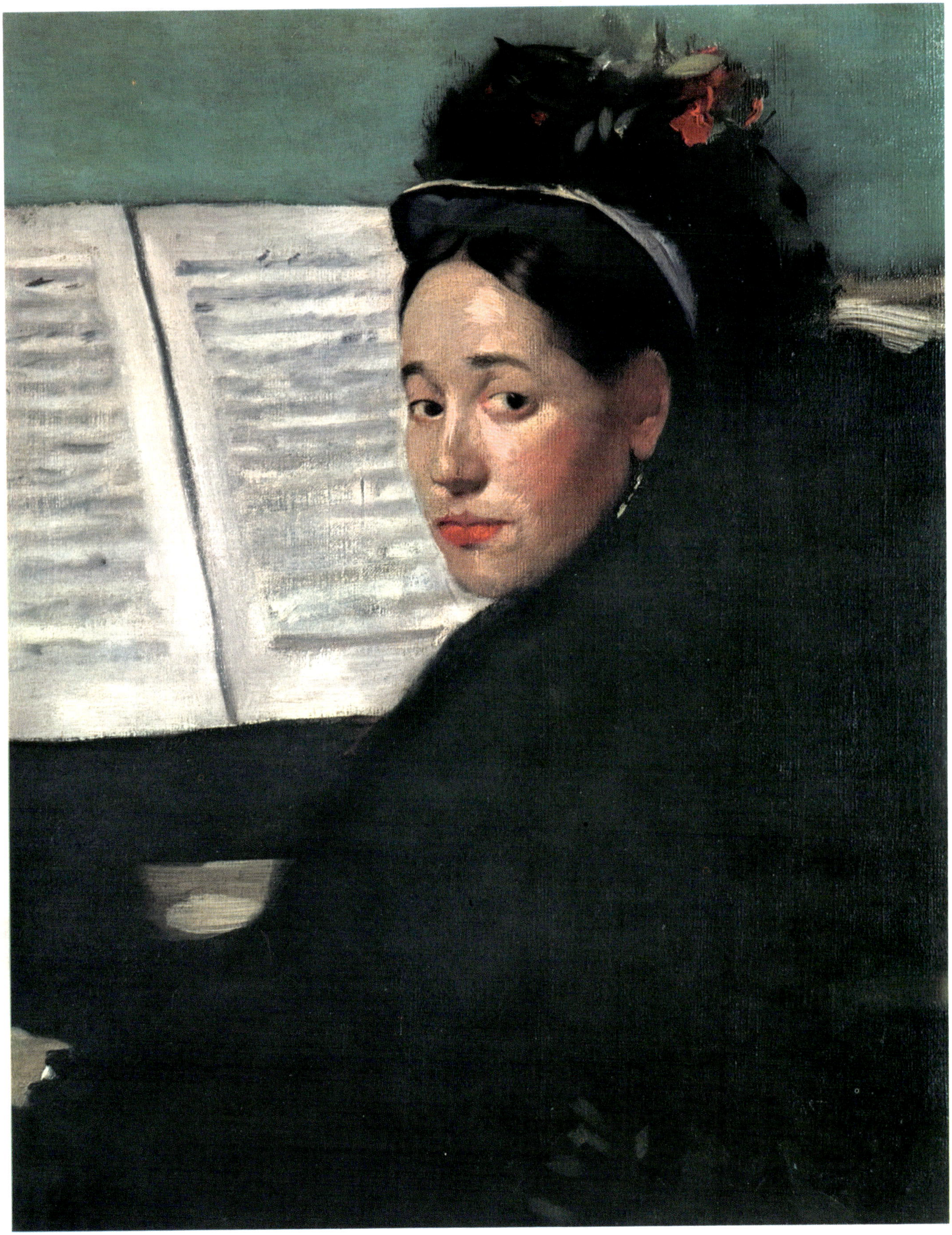

16

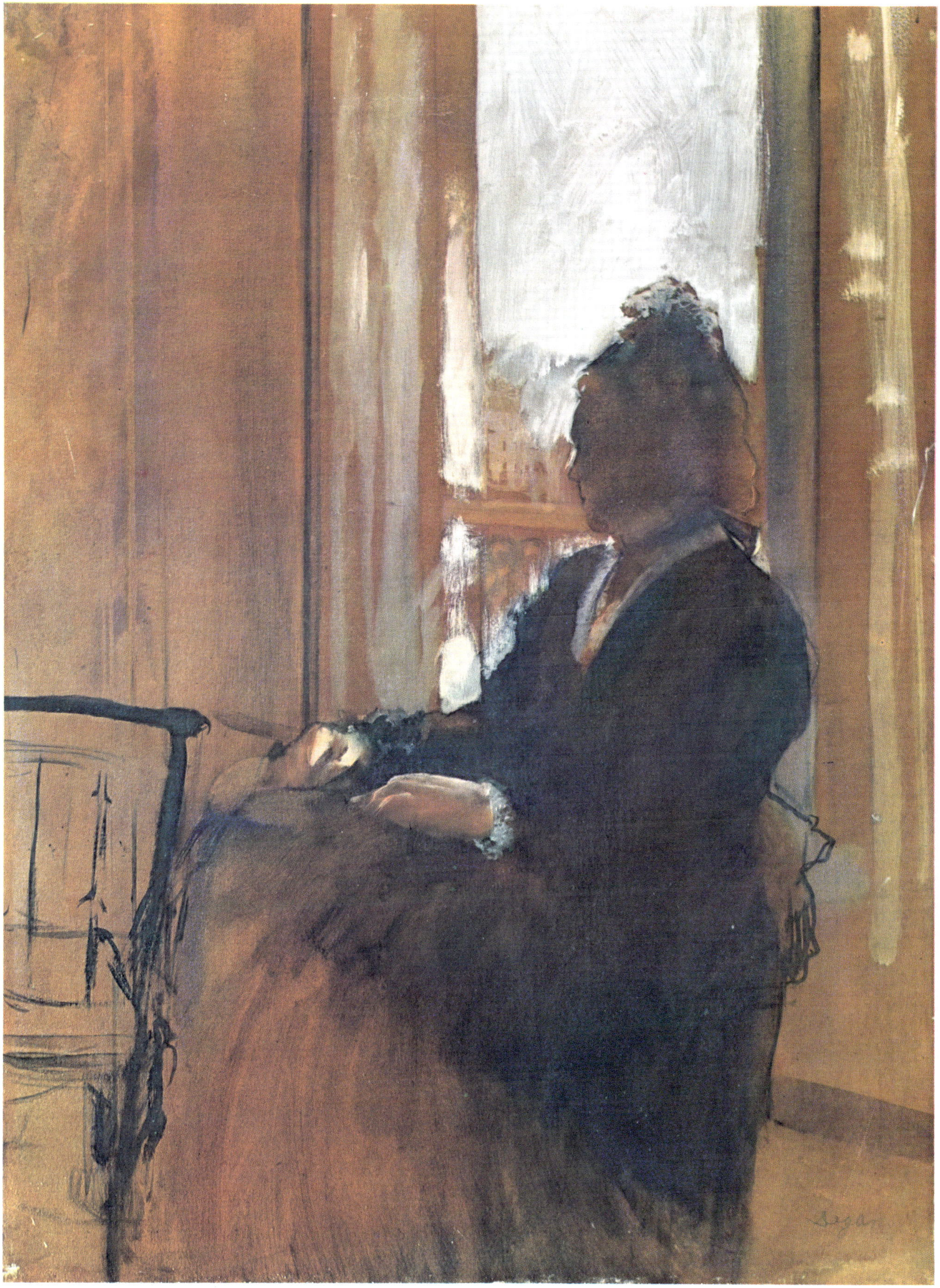
Degas

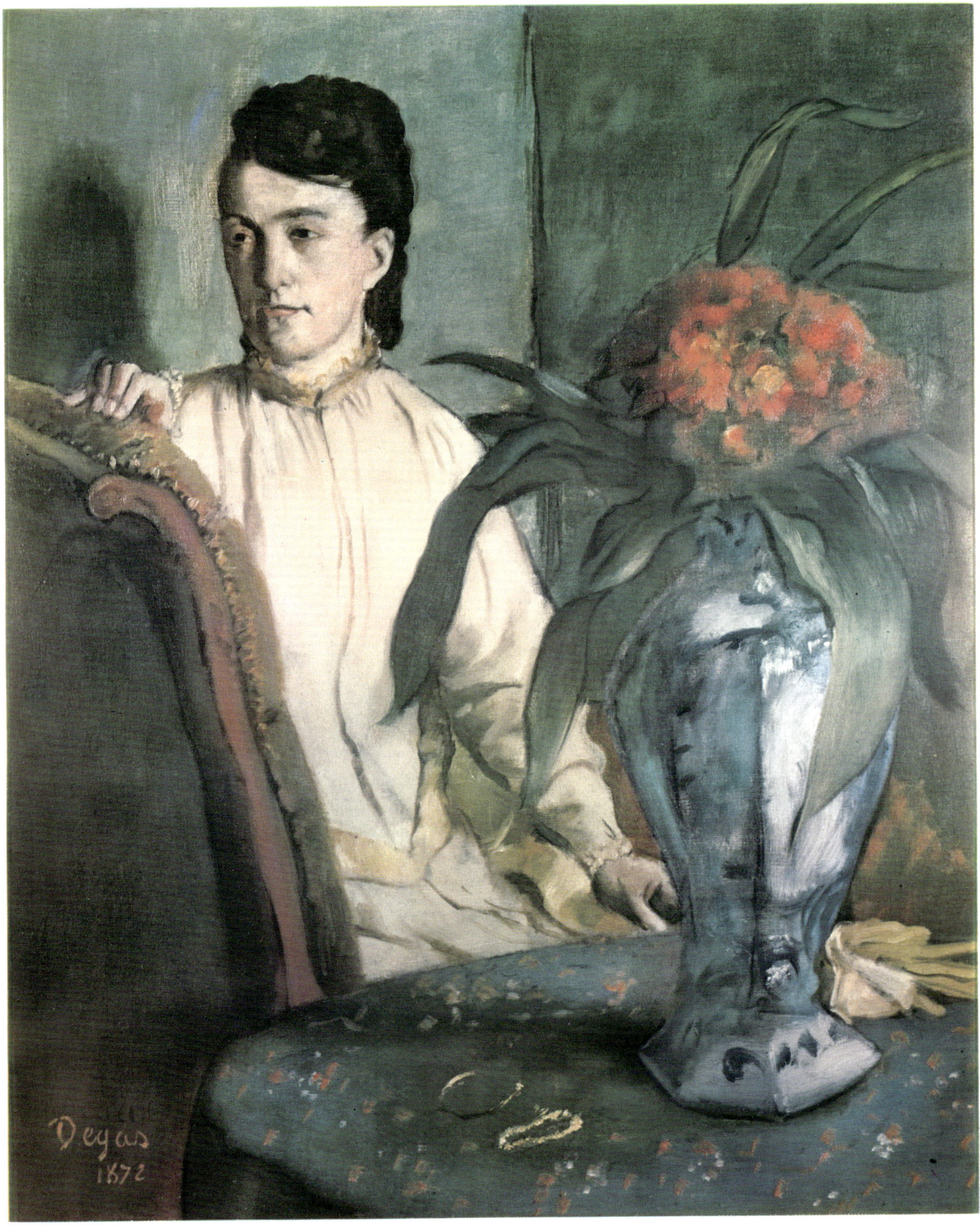
Degas
1872

19

20

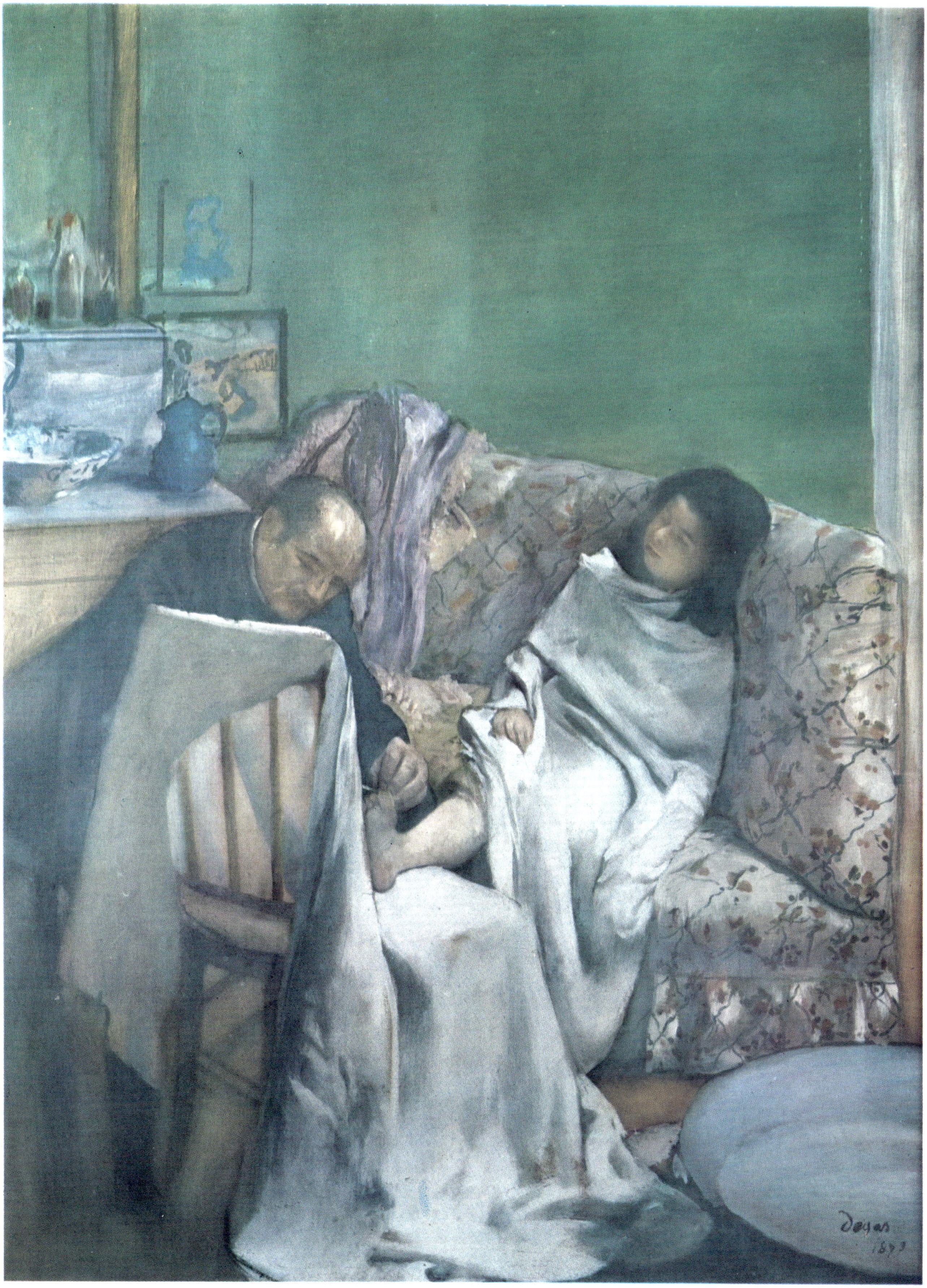
Degas
1873

22

23

24

25

26

27

28

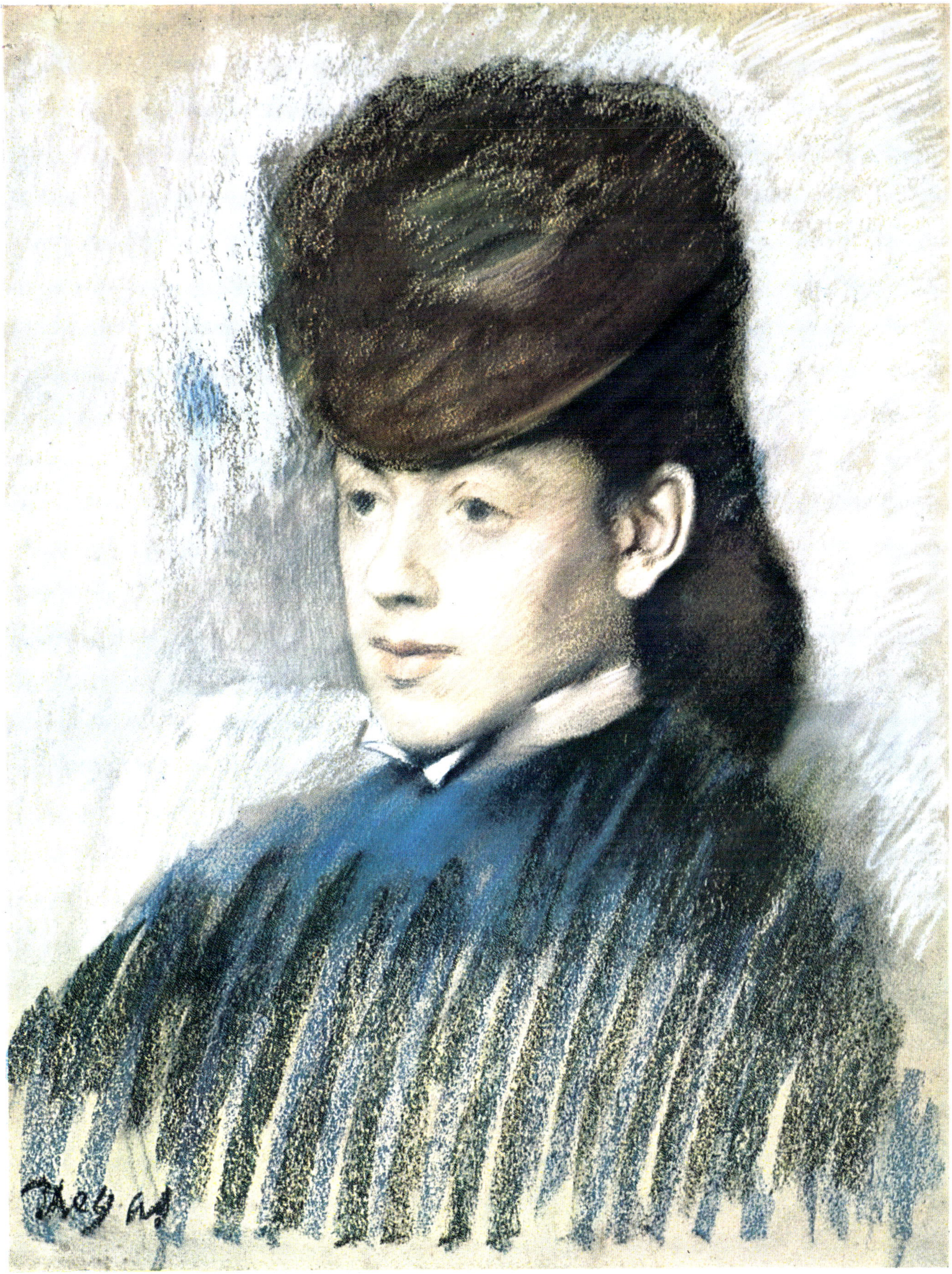

30

31

32

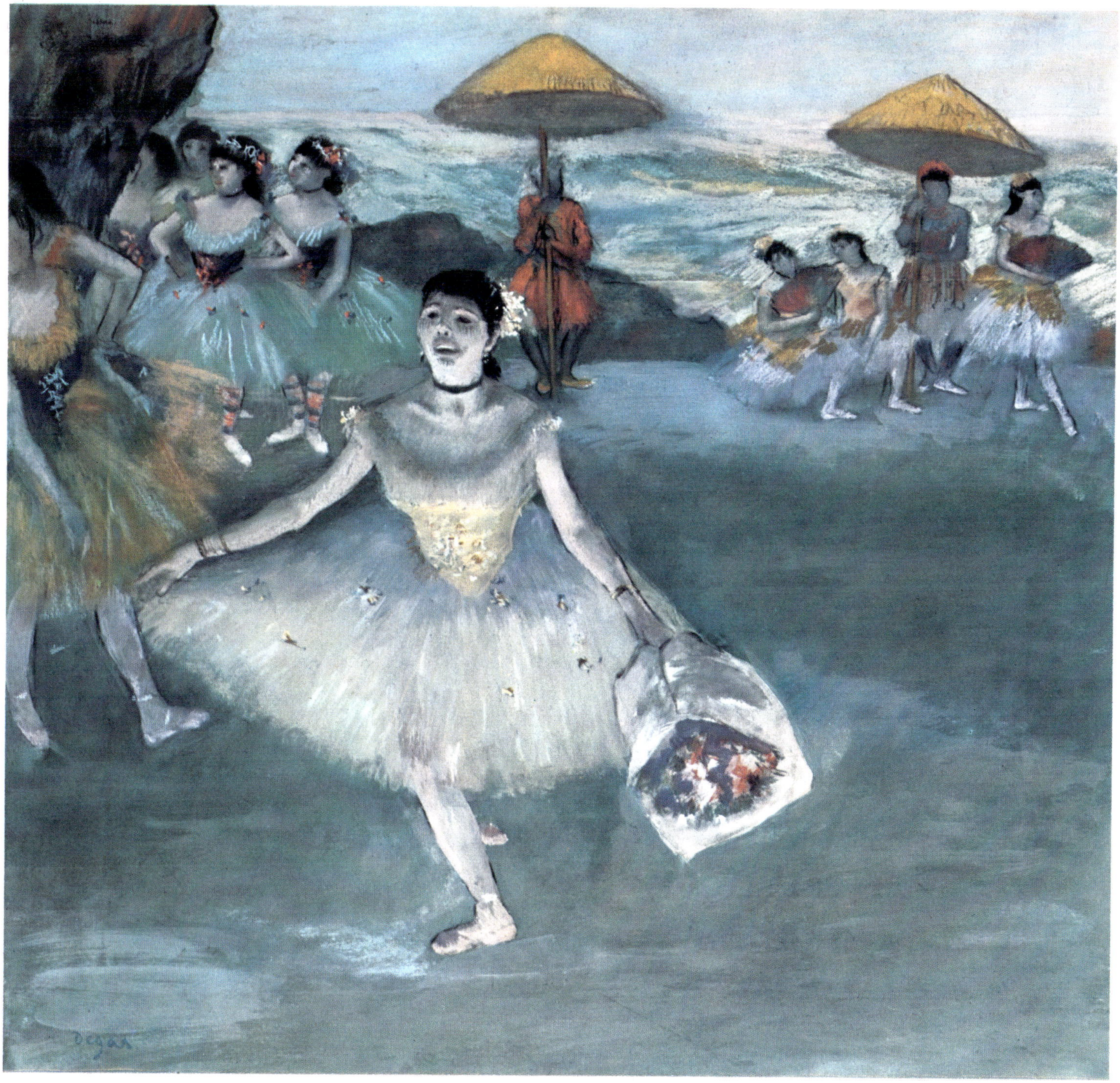
Degas

34

35

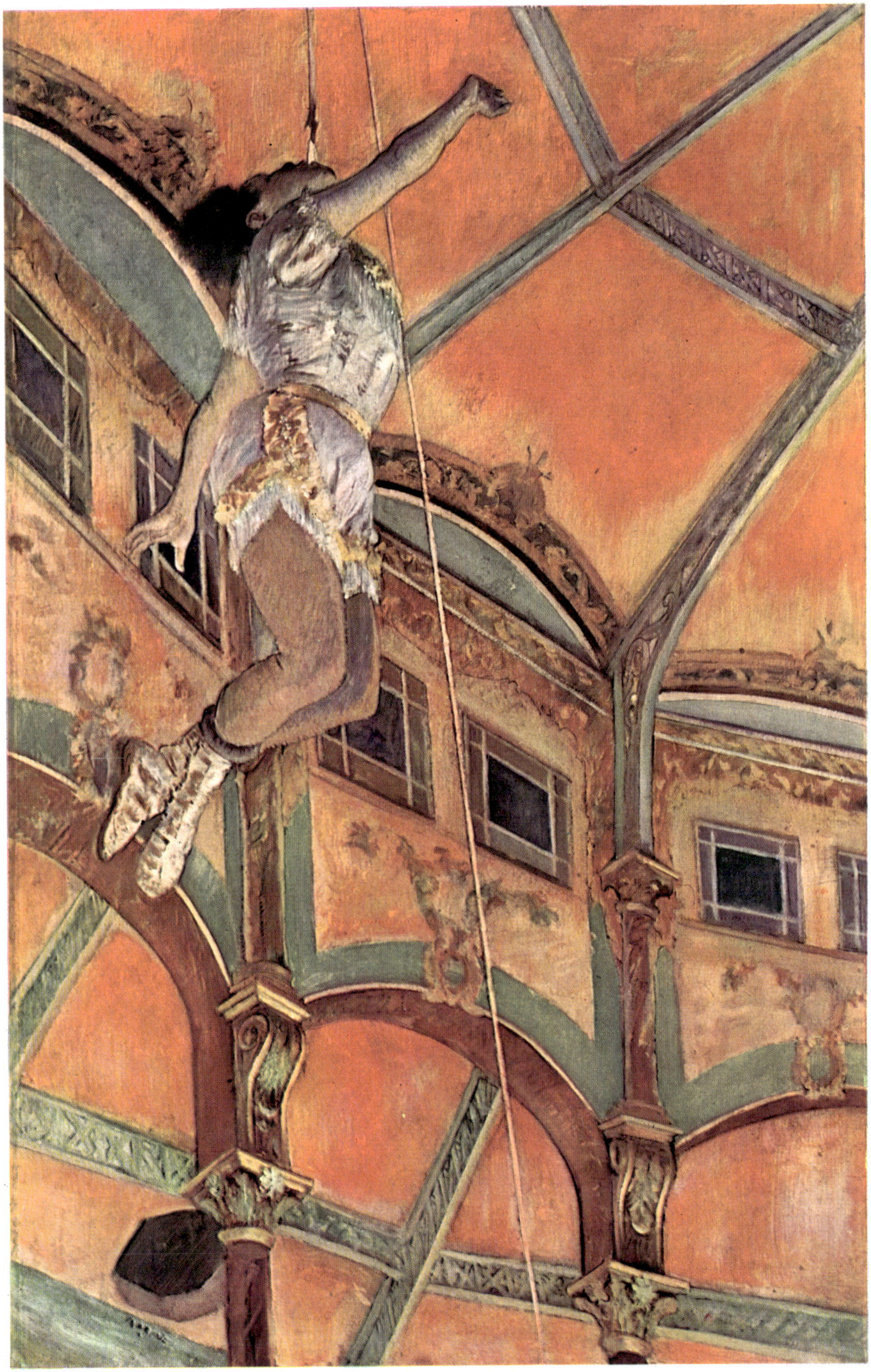

37

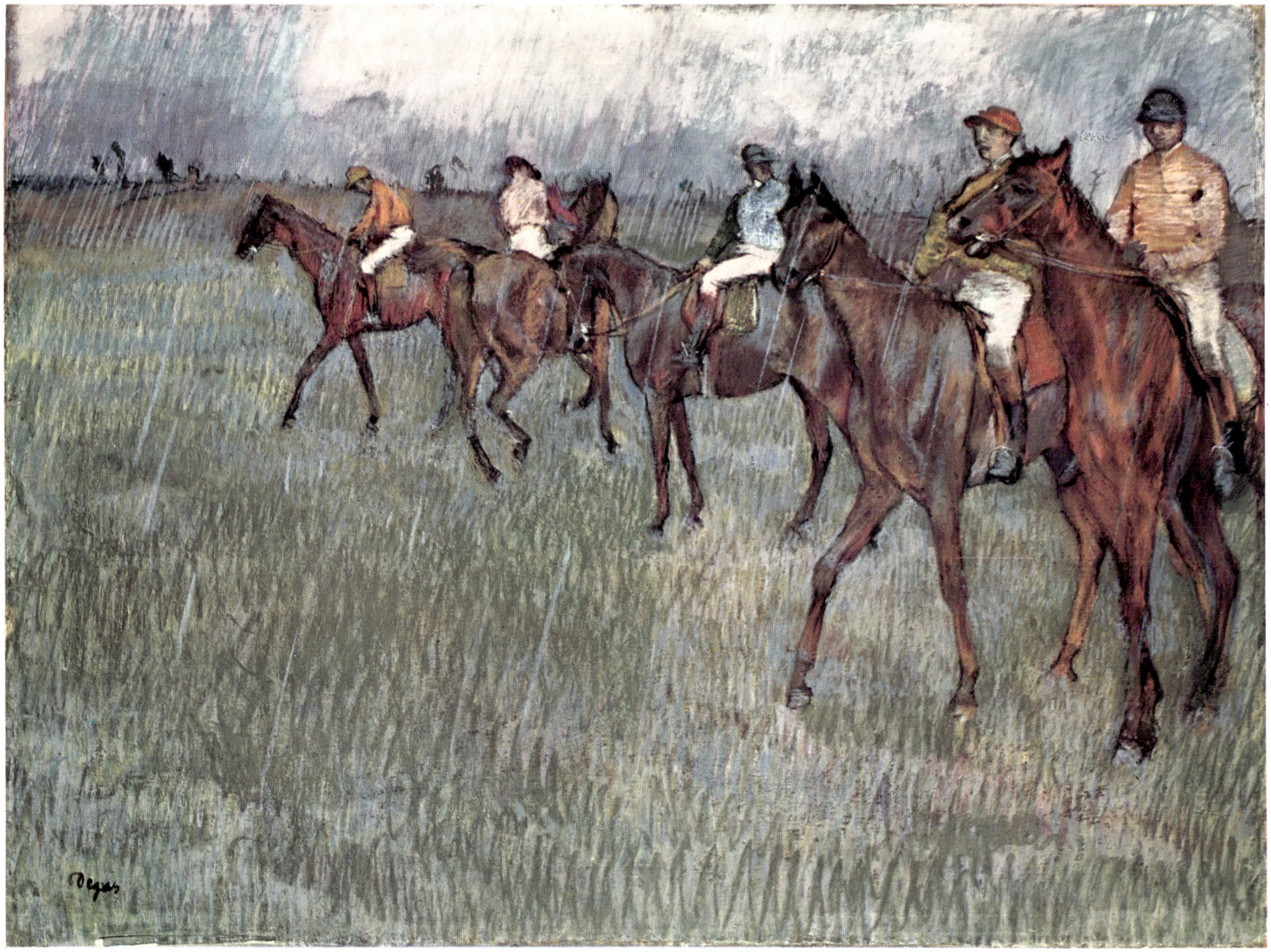

38

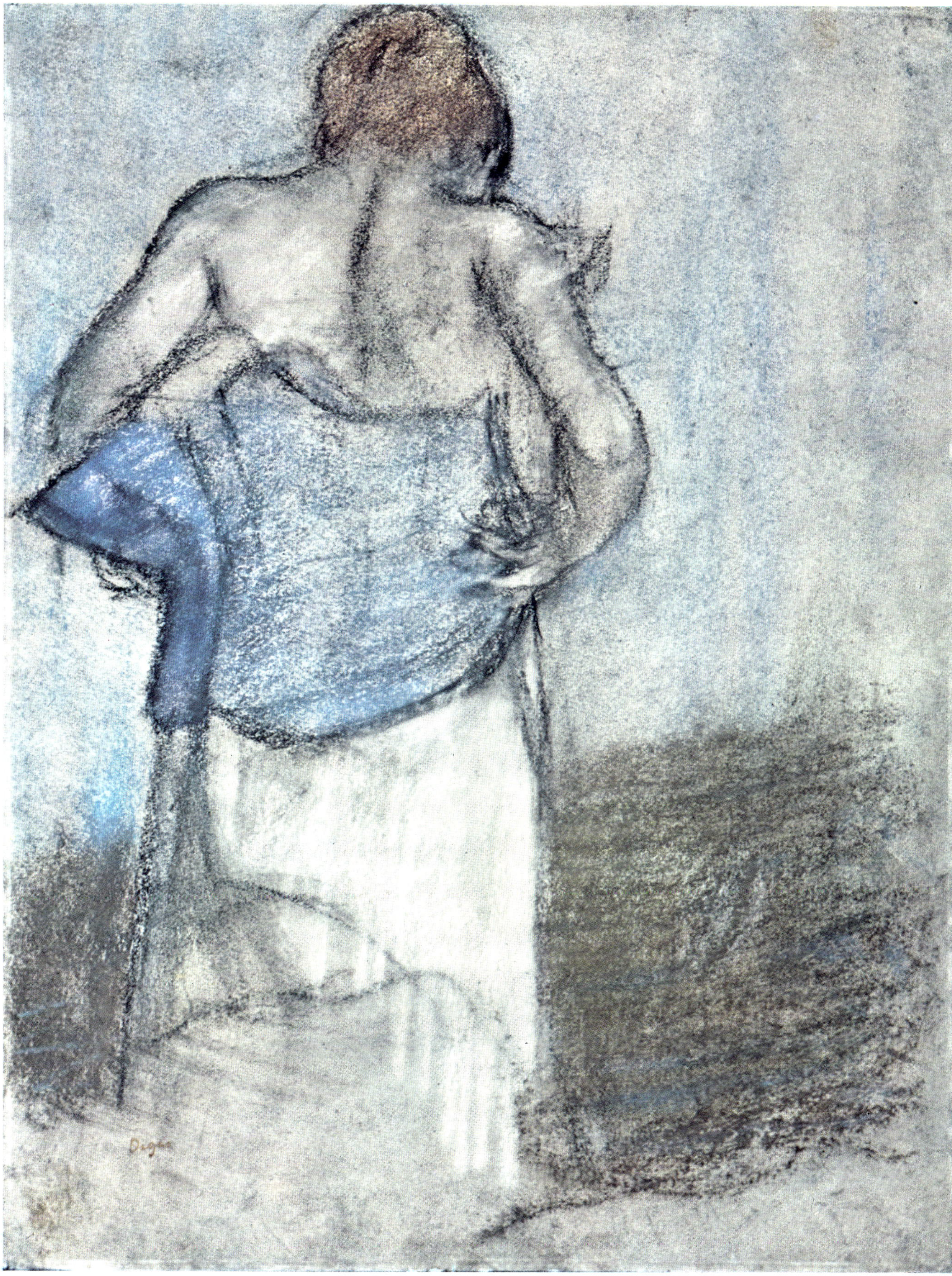
Degas

40

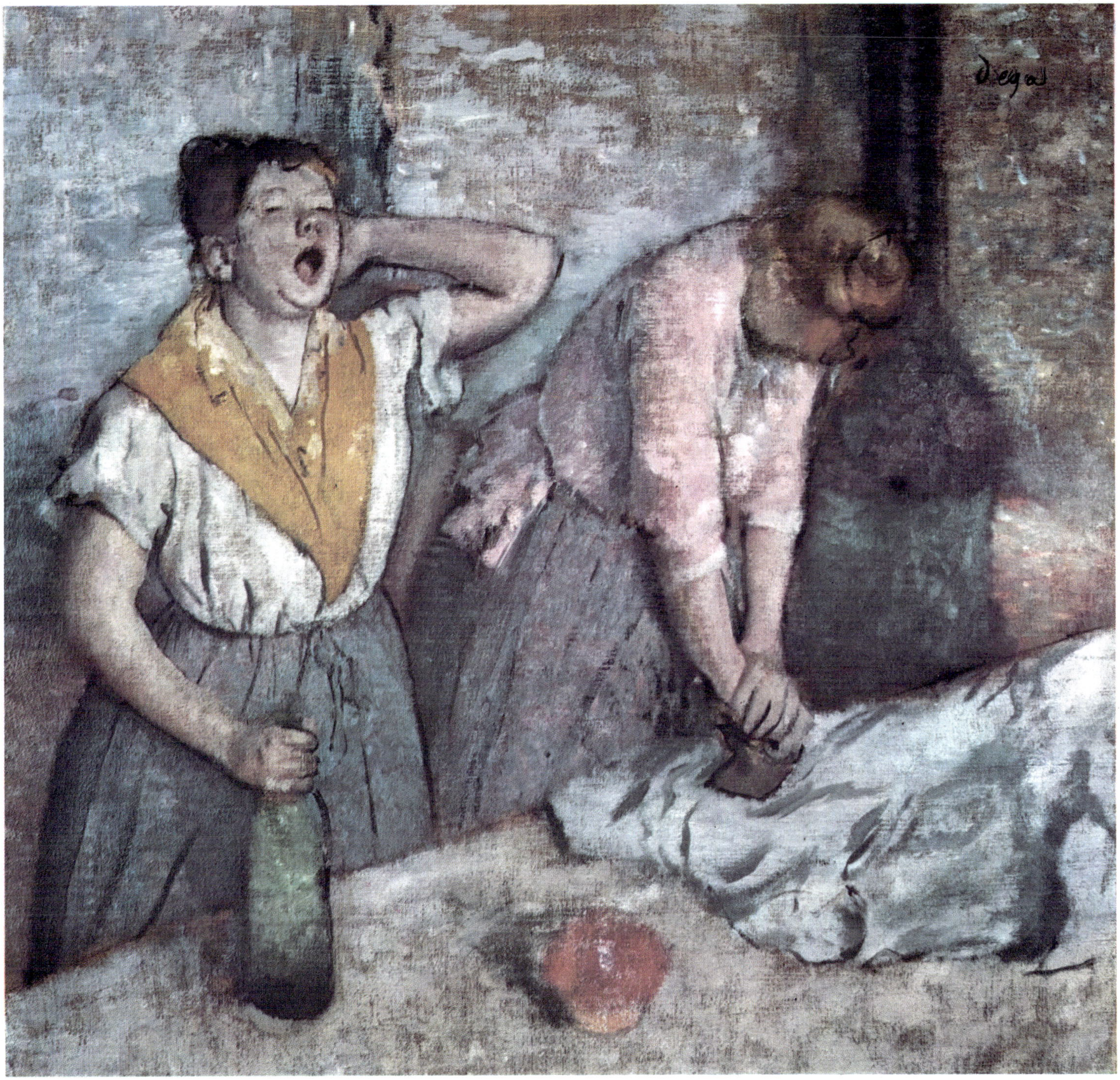

41

42

43

44

45

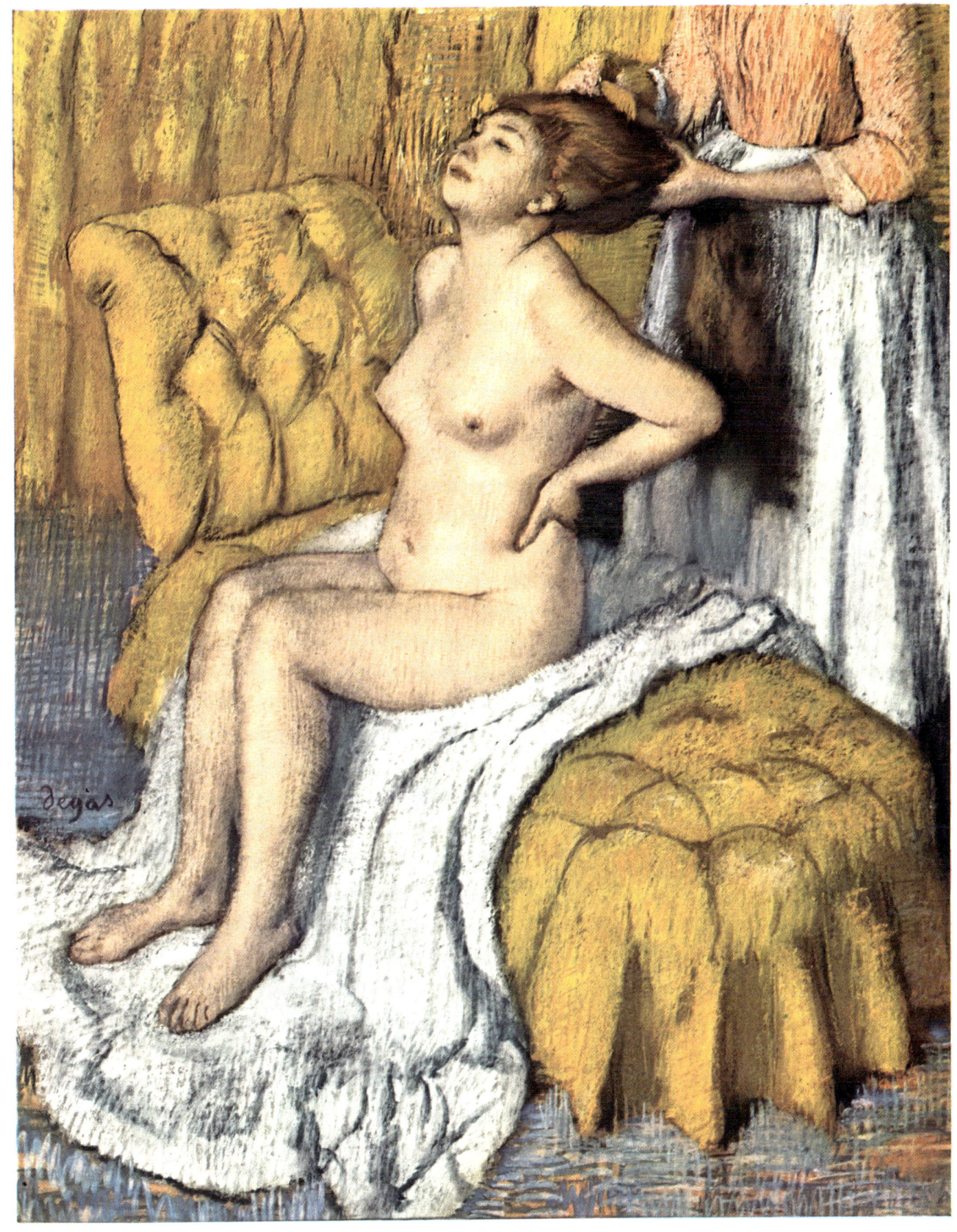

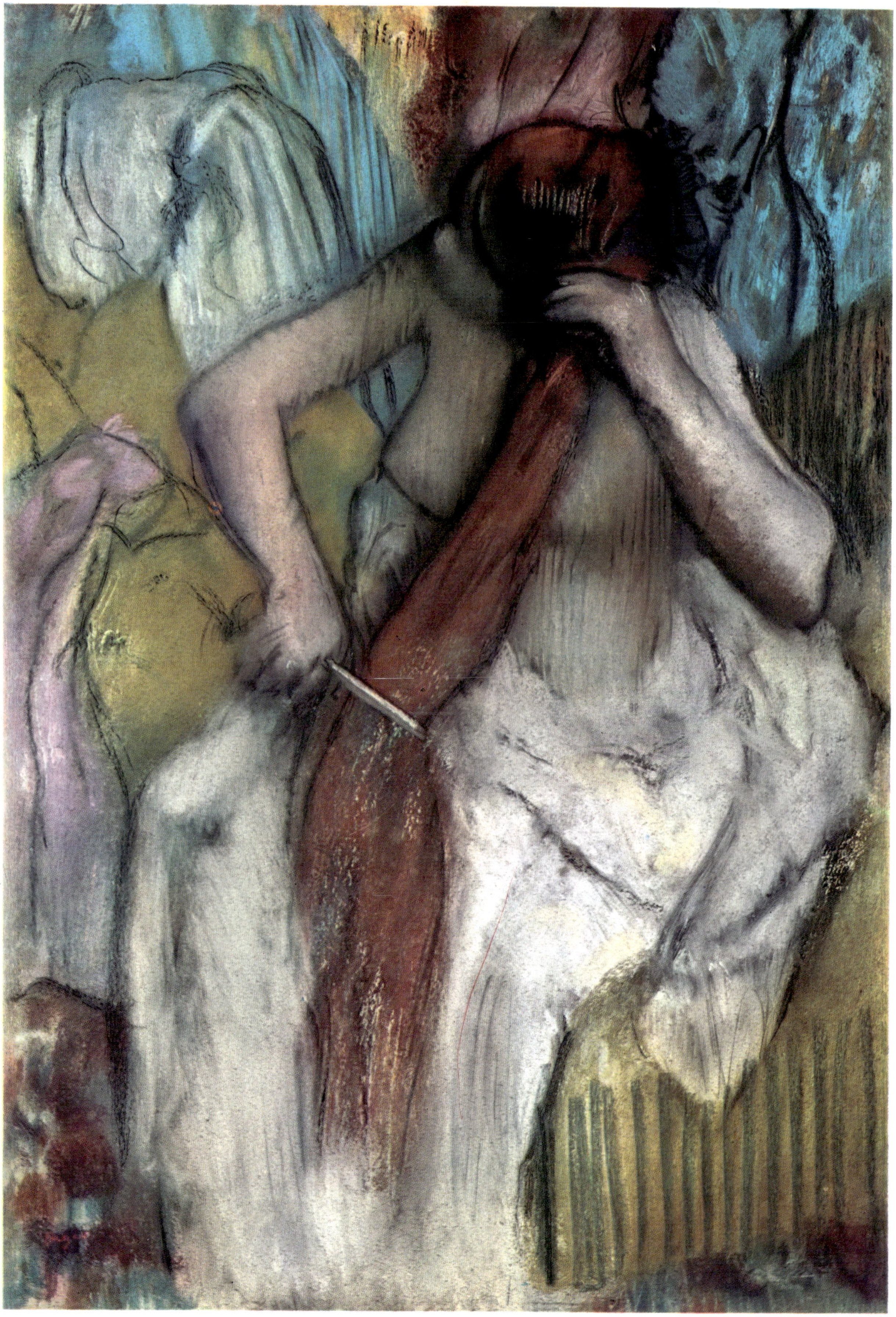

47

48